Brighton
Hidden Walks

Ric Morris

Published by Geographers'
A-Z Map Company Limited
An imprint of HarperCollins Publishers
Westerhill Road
Bishopbriggs
Glasgow
G64 2QT

HarperCollinsPublishers
Macken House, 39/40 Mayor Street Upper,
Dublin 1, D01 C9W8, Ireland

www.az.co.uk
a-z.maps@harpercollins.co.uk

1st edition 2023

A catalogue record for this book
is available from the British Library.

ISBN 978-0-00-856495-7

10 9 8 7 6 5 4 3 2 1

Printed in India

contents

introduction

Brighton is colourful, fun and a little bit naughty. As the nearest south coast resort to London, the city combines the traditional seaside resort with a cosmopolitan buzz usually reserved for much larger cities.

The small fishing town once known as Brighthelmstone first welcomed visitors from the 1750s when it became a fashionable sea-bathing health resort. One visitor, Prince George (who became the Prince Regent, then later King George IV), built one of Britain's most extravagant buildings, the Royal Pavilion, and set the tone of Brighton as a place of escape, pleasure and eccentricity. In the 19th century, the railways opened up the town to mass tourism and expansion.

Today, Brighton and Hove, as it is officially known, is a year-round city of commuters, tech and creative industries, students, celebrities, and is famous as Britain's LGBTQ+ capital.

Many people are familiar with the Brighton of day trips: the Palace Pier, Lanes and Royal Pavilion. Yet the city is full of hidden surprises which we will explore on these walks: from quirky backstreets and hidden histories to world-class architecture and atmospheric urban villages.

Geographically, Brighton is squeezed between the English Channel and the South Downs National Park – which means as well as the sea, you are a walk or easy bus ride away from rolling green hills. So this book also aims to entice you into the delights of downland and coastal Sussex on the doorstep of this unique and rewarding little city.

about the author

Ric Morris is a professional Blue Badge Tourist Guide in South East England, London and Brighton, where he runs *Only in Brighton!* tours. He has a background in English language and speech training. He lives in Hove.

how to use this book

Each of the 20 walks in this guide is set out in a similar way. They are all introduced with a brief description, including notes on things you will encounter on your walk, and a photograph of a place of interest you might pass along the way.

On the first page of each walk there is a panel of information outlining the distance of the walk, a guide to the walking time, and a brief description of the path conditions or the terrain you will encounter. A suggested starting point along with the nearest postcode is shown, although postcodes can cover a large area therefore this is just a rough guide.

The major part of each section is taken up with route maps and detailed point-to-point directions for the walk. The route instructions are prefixed by a number in a circle, and the corresponding location is shown on the map.

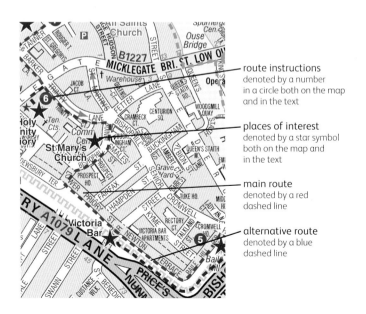

route instructions
denoted by a number
in a circle both on the map
and in the text

places of interest
denoted by a star symbol
both on the map and
in the text

main route
denoted by a red
dashed line

alternative route
denoted by a blue
dashed line

A·Z walk one

Seawater Cures, India and Royalty

City centre highlights and hidden delights.

This short walk starts at Royal Albion Hotel, occupying the site where it all began: the surgery that stood here in the 1750s was that of Dr Richard Russell, whose seawater cures transformed a quiet fishing town into a fashionable resort. Our tour takes in locations associated with King George IV, who first visited the town as a young prince in 1783 and continued his patronage throughout his regency and reign. The first of these is the site of the therapeutic baths pioneered by the Indian surgeon, Sake Dean Mohamed. Continuing the bathing theme, we pass the home of the 'queen of dippers', Martha Gunn.

George IV's Royal Pavilion – Indian outside and (sort of) Chinese inside – is surely Britain's most extravagant building. Next to it stands India Gate, which commemorates the Pavilion's use as a hospital for Indian soldiers during the First World War, while the surrounding Royal Pavilion Gardens is a supreme example of a restored Regency garden.

Opposite the Pavilion is Brighton Dome: built as royal stables, it is now a centre for culture. Completing our tour of the Cultural Quarter, we pass the Theatre Royal, built in honour of George in 1807, and the handsome Chapel Royal (check out their concerts), a fruitless attempt to entice the prince to prayer. Returning to Old Steine, once the best address in Brighton, we can admire the home of Maria Fitzherbert (Prince George's secret and illegal wife) and the hotel visited by George's brother and successor, William IV.

start / finish	Royal Albion Hotel, Old Steine
nearest postcode	BN1 1NT
distance	1¼ miles / 2 km
time	30 minutes
terrain	Surfaced roads and paths, some uneven paving, short cobbled section, some grass (optional).

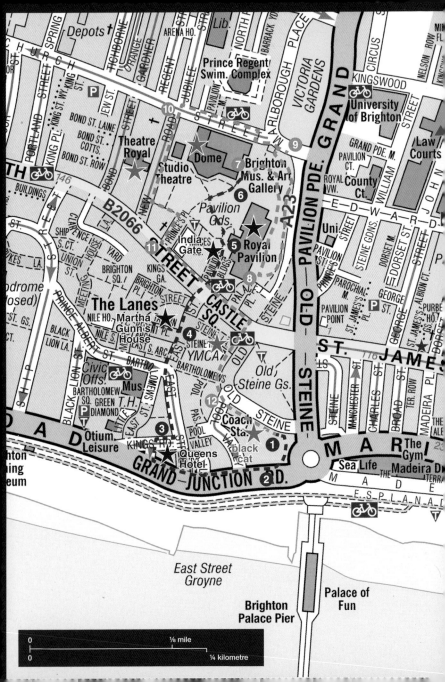

1 Start by the entrance of Royal Albion Hotel on the Old Steine (pronounced *steen*). Facing the entrance, walk left and round towards the sea, with the hotel on your right. When you reach the pedestrian crossing (don't cross!), look right to see the stone plaque on the side of the hotel to Dr Richard Russell, whose seawater cures first brought visitors to Brighton.

2 Stay on the right-hand side of the road and walk along Grand Junction Road. Cross three small side roads to reach the end of the line of buildings. Turn right to see the porch entrance to Queens Hotel ★ . By the door, note the blue plaque to Sake Dean Mohamed, 'Shampooing Surgeon to George IV and William IV'. Walk round to the north side, keeping the hotel on your right, and cross Kings Road when you can. When you join East Street, turn left.

3 Walk up East Street, with its shops and restaurants, for nearly 200 yards (180 metres). Continue ahead onto the pedestrian area. Just before the taxi rank, the street opens out onto a small square with restaurants and cafés. Head to the far left (northwest) corner to find a characteristic 18th-century Brighton-style black and white cottage, now a café. This was the home of Martha Gunn ★ , the famous 'dipper' who helped visitors into the sea – spot her faded stone plaque to the right of the door.

4 Return to East Street and turn left to continue past the taxi rank. Cross North Street at the pedestrian crossing to the left of the mini-roundabout and continue forwards to India Gate ★ – given in thanks for Brighton's role in treating Indian soldiers injured during the First World War, including Mir Dast, awarded a Victoria Cross and remembered with a plaque outside the Royal Pavilion Shop to your right. The shop is worth a visit for its exotic souvenirs and local information.

5 Walk past the gate into the Royal Pavilion Gardens. The visitor entrance to the Prince Regent's pleasure palace, the Royal Pavilion ★ , is on your right. Bear slightly left to follow the path into the middle of the gardens. At the junction, take the path to the right, with views left to Brighton Dome ★ (former royal stables, now concert halls).

6 At the next junction of paths near the flower beds on the right, look for a glass circle set into the path. There is a line of these circles running right to left connecting the Pavilion with the Dome. These are the skylights of a tunnel used by Prince George to visit his horses.

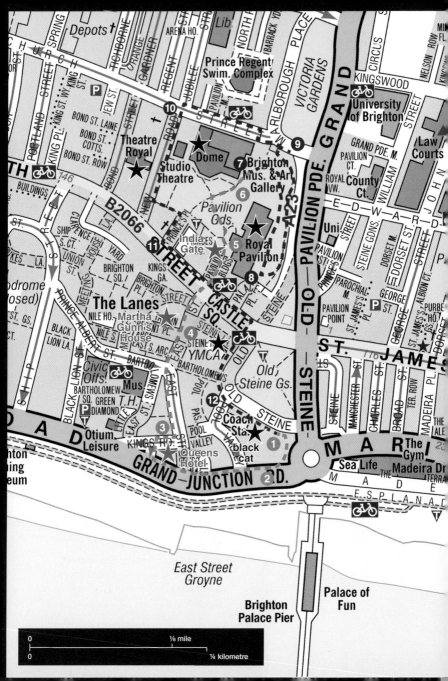

7 Continue past Brighton Museum & Art Gallery towards the North Gate, commissioned by William IV in 1832. Just before you reach the gate, turn right onto the grass and head across to the other (east) side of the Royal Pavilion. If you prefer you can follow the paved path that runs just inside the perimeter wall. This quieter part of the gardens gives you the best views of the Pavilion.

8 When you reach the end of the gardens, turn round and head back the way you came, this time following the paved path on the right all the way to the North Gate. Turn right on to Marlborough Place to the statue of George IV (Prince Regent) opposite a statue of his niece Queen Victoria, the last monarch to own the Royal Pavilion.

9 Turning round, walk past North Gate to your left and up Church Street. Cross the road at the pedestrian crossing to give you more views of the former royal stables – now the Brighton Dome ★ concert halls. In the daytime the foyer is sometimes open for coffee.

10 At the next road junction (walk three starts here), turn left onto New Road and pass the Greek revival Unitarian Church. A little further on, at the beginning of the gardens on your left, note the statue of Brighton comedian Max Miller then the Theatre Royal ★ on your right. Near the end of New Road, just before the buildings on the left, take the path to re-enter the gardens. Take the first right into Prince's Place. At the end on the right-hand corner is the red brick Chapel Royal.

11 From Prince's Place, turn left following the busy North Street downhill all the way until you reach the traffic light junction with Old Steine. Turn right and follow the line of buildings to your right around Old Steine. Immediately after the alleyway, note the YMCA building ★ on your right, once the home of Mrs Fitzherbert, the secret and illegal wife of Prince George.

12 Follow the main road round as it swings left, taking care when crossing the side roads. On the south side of Old Steine is a large youth hostel with 'Royal York' on the porch. Note the plaque commemorating the stay of King William IV and Queen Adelaide when it was the Royal York Hotel. On the next building, spot the black cat sculpture ★ on the corner about halfway up. Continue ahead to the Royal Albion Hotel, where the walk finishes.

AZ walk two

Secrets of the Lanes

The atmospheric old town.

The Lanes is the old town of Brighton and has always been at the heart of the city. It is undoubtedly one of its most attractive areas: tiny cottages cluster around a warren of narrow alleyways once home to fishermen and their families, now vibrant with shops, cafés, restaurants and pubs.

Many of the buildings date back to the late 1700s, a time when Brighton was developing from a modest fishing town into a fashionable health resort for the rich. And here you can see the traditional building styles which characterized the area: small houses faced with flint, painted stucco, tiles (including 'mathematical' tiles) and even wood.

Among the quaint little cottages, there are some grander buildings, such as the imposing 1830s Brighton Town Hall and the Hippodrome theatre. There are also religious buildings, including a stunning synagogue, a Quaker meeting house and a former chapel.

But most of all, come to the Lanes to enjoy the atmosphere and the surprises around every corner and down each alleyway. Even though most visitors are familiar with this area, every visit will reveal a delightful new detail. Feel free to get lost and discover the Lanes in your own way, but, especially if you are short of time, this walk is the most efficient route to uncover the highlights and hidden corners of this magical quarter.

start / finish	Brighton Town Hall, Bartholomews
nearest postcode	BN1 1JW
distance	1 mile / 1.5 km
time	30 minutes
terrain	Paved roads, some uneven paving, one set of steps (optional).

Established in the Lanes
~ since 1914 ~
# DOYLES
ANTIQUE
JEWELLERS

CLASSIC
CHES WANTED
OR CASH
the Carter Patek Philippe

WANTED
Fine Diamond Jewellery
RINGS · BRACELETS · BROOCHES
NECKLACES · EARRINGS · ETC
Gold Wanted

New Secondhand Diamond and Gemset ·
Jewellery FOR SALE
Any Antique Diamond Jewellery FOR CASH

Fine Antique
JEWELLERY

Theatre
Royal

Studio
Theatre

Dome

Brighton
Mus. & Art
Gallery

PAVILION
CT.

ROYAL
VW.

Co

NEW

Pavilion
Gds.

A23

PAVILION PDE.

Uni.

STREET

PRINCE'S PL.

PRINCES
HO.

Royal
Pavilion

E — D

PAVILION
ST.

PRINCE'S

8

ST.

PAROCH
M.

Puget's
Cottage

STANSL.

9

KINGS
GA.

BRIGHTON
PL.

PAVILION
BLDGS.

PALACE
PL.

STEINE

OLD

PAVILION
POINT

ST. JAMES

STREET

CASTLE
SQ.

1

Lanes

7

TAVERN

REGENT PL.

10

STEINE LA.

STEINE HO.

YMCA

ST.

PAVILION

MARKET

REGENT
ARCH

EAST S. ARC.

EAST

BARTHOLOMEWS

OLD

OLD

Old
Steine Gs.

STEINE

ST.

IS

BARTHO.

EAST ST. BARTHOLOMEWS

Mus.

H

1

11

POOL

PAS.

Coach
Sta.

STEINE

MANCHESTER

CT.

Quadrophenia
Alley

EAST ST.

KINGS RD.

POOL
VALLEY

POOL
VALLEY

BRILLS

M

M

Sea

GRAND JUNCTION RD.

2066

1 Starting at the front of Brighton Town Hall ★ and facing the road, head left up Prince Albert Street. At the next road junction you find two historic pubs, The Cricketers and The Black Lion. The Cricketers is on the site of a 16th-century inn, although the current building probably dates from the late 17th century. The Greene function room commemorates the author Graham Greene, who enjoyed drinking here, and the pub features in his novel *Travels with my Aunt*. The Black Lion on the left was reconstructed in 1974 on the site of a 16th-century brewery.

2 Walk down the alleyway between the two pubs. Continue across the road to the next passage, Ship Street Gardens, with some hidden gardens and a couple of small shops. At the end turn left onto Middle Street until you come to the distinctive building on the left with pale bricks and coloured arches. This is Middle Street Synagogue ★ , one of the finest 19th-century synagogues in the country. No longer used for regular worship, it is occasionally open for visitors.

3 Turn back up Middle Street, this time on the left-hand pavement. On the wall of number 20 note the stone plaque to William Friese-Greene ★ , a movie camera inventor who, in 1905, patented one of the earliest colour film systems. To your right, you can see the Hippodrome theatre. Built in 1897 and closed in 2006, it was Brighton's main theatre for popular entertainment. Acts included Laurel and Hardy, Harry Houdini and the Beatles. At the time of writing it is being restored.

4 Continue to the top of Middle Street. At the junction with Duke Street, look straight ahead to see the gap in the buildings, Dukes Yard. This is a private area, but if you look through the gate you can see 37a Duke Street ★ on the left, an unusual 18th-century white cottage faced with wood blocks designed to imitate stone.

5 Retrace your steps to walk a short distance back down Middle Street, this time taking the first left into Dukes Lane, a 1979 take on traditional Brighton architecture. At the end, cross the road and turn right and very soon on your left you will see the garden in front of Friends Meeting House ★ , a Quaker place of worship since 1805. Feel free to enjoy the garden, and the Meeting House often hosts markets, concerts and talks.

6 Leaving the garden, turn right and walk up Ship Street. Take the next right down Union Street. You are now in the heart of the Lanes. On the left is the former Union Chapel ★ , now a pub, built in the late 1600s as Brighton's first legal place of worship outside the Church of England. Turn right after the chapel/pub and follow the lane as it turns left then right again. Continue walking for a few metres then take the long alleyway on the left that runs slightly downhill. This is one of the most attractive lanes in the heart of the jewellery quarter.

7 At the end, when you emerge onto Brighton Place, turn left. Then after the pub turn left again and you will come out into the small Brighton Square, a 1960s version of the Lanes. Turn right then left to exit the square by the opposite corner. At the end turn right into Meeting House Lane, then take the next right into Hanningtons Lane, the latest addition to the Lanes, opened in 2019 on the site of a former service area.

8 Where the lane opens out at a junction, note Puget's Cottage ★ next to the steps. One of the oldest functioning domestic buildings in Brighton, dating from around 1700, it was hidden and largely forgotten until Hanningtons Lane was built. Take the lane to the right to return to Brighton Place.

9 Immediately turn left down the hill, then right up Market Street past some small restaurants to emerge onto an open area, also called Market Street. On your right note the Pump House pub, with its facade of 'mathematical' tiles – a cheap alternative to bricks, found chiefly in East Sussex and Kent. Head left downhill through the short passage which brings you out onto East Street.

10 Turn right down East Street. Roughly halfway to the sea (about 110 yards or 100 metres), look for a small alleyway on the right next to number 11. Quadrophenia Alley ★ featured in the 1979 movie *Quadrophenia*, about the Mod youth subculture, and the alley has become a place of pilgrimage with fans adding their name to the wall. Walk down this alley until you emerge onto Little East Street.

11 Ahead is Brighton Town Hall ★ – its basement holds the fascinating Police Cells Museum, which is open on certain days for pre-booked visits. Walk up the steps in front of you (or take the step-free route round to the right of the building), then turn right to return to the start.

A·Z walk three

Shops and Street Art

The eccentric soul of the city in North Laine.

There's nowhere quite like North Laine. Occupying the area between the railway station and the Lanes, North Laine could be described as the heart and soul of Brighton: at its core are over three hundred independent shops, along with buzzing cafés, restaurants and pubs. But the lesser-known outlying streets are also richly rewarding, with multi-coloured houses and converted warehouses, many of which are adorned with commissioned murals or unofficial graffiti (including a Banksy).

As every local likes to tell you, North Laine is not the same as the Lanes (see walk two). *Laine* is an old Sussex word for arable land – the old strip field boundaries survive in the grid of narrow streets – which was developed in the early 1800s as Brighton expanded northwards to accommodate light industry and workers' housing. Run down by the 1970s, North Laine was saved from demolition, heralding its regeneration into the city's brightest, funkiest and… well… *most Brighton*, quarter. Perhaps the biggest success story of North Laine is Body Shop, which opened its first store here in 1976.

Although this is a short walk, you could easily spend a few hours here, snooping around the unique shops, taking in the architectural details, exploring little side streets and café-hopping, while in the evening you can see an art-house movie or a comedy show, or drink at some of the city's best-loved pubs.

start / finish	Junction of Church Street and Jubilee Street
nearest postcode	BN1 1UD
distance	1¼ miles / 2 km
time	30 minutes
terrain	Paved roads, no steps.

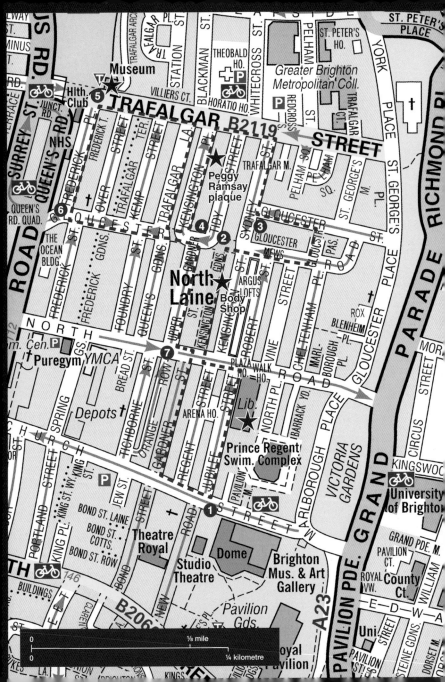

1 Starting at the corner of Church Street and Jubilee Street, walk down Jubilee Street. In the square note Jubilee Library ★ , which has won awards for its design and sustainability. At the end of the street, turn left onto North Road. Cross North Road at the pedestrian lights and proceed into the narrow shopping alleyway of Kensington Gardens. Approaching the end of Kensington Gardens there is a plaque on the wall of number 22 indicating the site of the world's first Body Shop ★ , founded by Anita Roddick in 1976.

2 At the end, turn right down Gloucester Road. Here you can get a glimpse of North Laine's industrial past in the old warehouses, now homes and offices. Immediately after The Eagle pub, turn left and head for the small passageway through the houses, then turn left up Gloucester Street.

3 At the end of the street turn right along another lively shopping street, then turn left at the T-junction into Trafalgar Street and take the second left into Kensington Place. This is very much a street of two sides – uniform urban terraces on the left and a jumble of cottage gardens on the right. On the left at number 34 is a blue plaque commemorating theatrical agent Peggy Ramsay ★ , who represented leading playwrights including David Hare and Joe Orton.

4 At the end turn right then right again into Trafalgar Lane, which displays some of the best examples of the city's street art and graffiti. Be aware of vehicles as the street narrows. At the end turn left and continue up Trafalgar Street until you reach the junction with Frederick Place next to the pub. Diagonally opposite just under the bridge is the Toy and Model Museum ★ . (If you continue up the hill, walk nine starts at Brighton Station.)

5 Cross to the far side of Frederick Place to get a view of the side of the pub and the large mural depicting late rock icons, a project led by local artist REQ. At the bottom, in the frame, you can also see Banksy's *Kissing Coppers*, a faithful copy of the 2004 original which was removed from here and sold in Miami for $575,000.

6 Continue along Frederick Place and turn left at the junction. Proceed along Gloucester Road, taking the right turn into Upper Gardner Street, which hosts a flea market every Saturday.

7 At the end turn left then almost immediately right into Gardner Street, crossing North Road at the pedestrian lights just beyond the turning. Gardner Street is lined with interesting and eccentrically decorated shops. At the end turn left, which will take you back to the start.

AZ walk four

Twittens and Bungaroosh

A circuit of backstreet alleyways.

Away from the busy streets, you can experience the city centre from a fresh angle along a route almost entirely of *twittens* – the old Sussex word for an alleyway. Each twitten has its own atmosphere, from half-forgotten service areas to hidden rows of neat residential cottages lined with well-kept gardens, so even if you know Brighton well, this short walk can feel like an urban adventure.

Here the traditional building materials of Brighton are on display. *Bungaroosh* is the local term for a rough composite of flint, pebbles and broken brick which is generally disguised with render or tiles at the front of buildings, but our walk takes us round the back where the bungaroosh is often exposed, along with more familiar-looking walls of flint and brick.

Our route circles Brighton Railway Station, with dramatic views from above and below, and the adjoining former industrial area, where locomotives and, later, cars were once manufactured. This area has now been rebuilt with flats and offices, but there are reminders of the old locomotive sidings, notably in the modern take on the twitten, the Brighton Greenway wild corridor.

This trail also passes some of Brighton's best pubs, so feel free to stop for a drink or two along the way.

start / finish	Junction of Duke Street and Ship Street
nearest postcode	BN1 1AG
distance	2¼ miles / 3.6 km
time	1 hour
terrain	Surfaced roads and footpaths, some narrow passageways, some uneven and cobbled surfaces, some hills and steps.

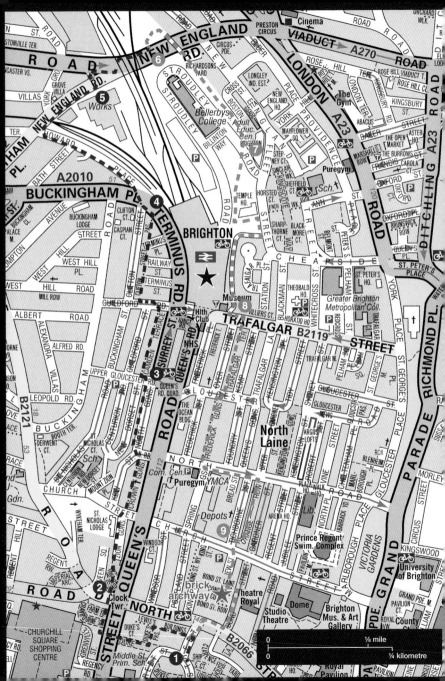

1 With the former church – a gallery at the time of writing – on your left, walk north up Ship Street. Look for an opening on your left to your first twitten, Lewis's Buildings. Follow this passage to the end where it turns left to emerge onto Duke Street, then turn right. At the busy West Street, cross at the pedestrian lights and turn right, then go over the crossroads at the traffic lights, passing the clock tower (built to commemorate Queen Victoria's Golden Jubilee and displaying portraits of Victoria's family).

2 Walk a short distance up Queen's Road and take the first left onto Air Street then immediately turn right up Zion Gardens. Note the exposed walls on your right – these are good examples of the rough building material known locally as bungaroosh. Cross the road at the end, bearing slightly left, to enter the next alleyway, Crown Gardens. At the end, continue ahead along North Gardens.

3 At the end of North Gardens, cross to the far side, turn left then immediately right into Camden Terrace, which has an almost Mediterranean atmosphere with its attractive whitewashed cottages. At the end, cross to the far side, turn left up the hill then turn right into Clifton Street Passage. Where the passage opens out to the right, there are views over the great glass and iron canopy of Brighton Station ★ .

4 When you emerge onto Terminus Road, take great care when crossing this busy road and continue ahead onto Howard Place. From here there are views over the valley and the station, and you can appreciate the engineering achievement of situating a railway station halfway up a steep hill! At the end of Howard Place, turn right down New England Road.

5 Shortly before the road goes under a large railway bridge, cross the road at the traffic lights, then immediately turn right to cross again to a central reservation. Follow the pavement round to the right and cross at another set of lights. When you reach the far side turn right, so that you are walking down the left-hand side of New England Road, beneath the railway bridge.

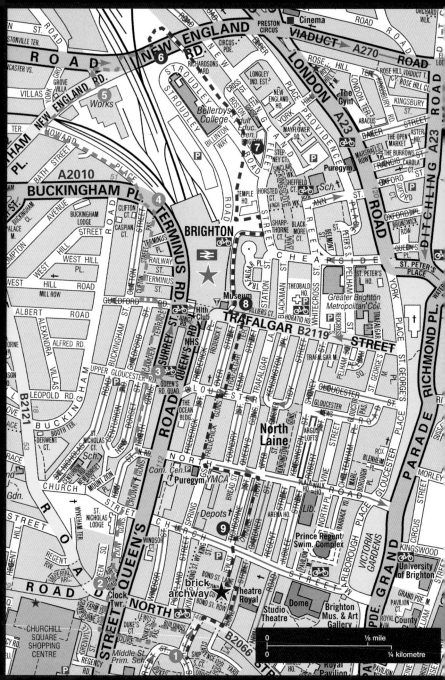

6 After the railway bridge, look left for a gap in the wall, with an information board indicating the entrance to the Greenway. Walk up the steps and follow the path as you cross an old railway bridge with the Ghost Train sculpture, a reminder of the Jenny Lind locomotives that ran on the Brighton line from 1847. This path continues along the route of a former railway siding serving the Brighton locomotive works (1850s to 1950s).

7 At the end of the path, cross Stroudley Road and continue ahead, taking the small set of steps up to the path between the buildings (NOT the steep steps on your right). When you reach the road at the top and Brighton Station comes into view, take the long flight of steps down to your left (or take the lift), then turn right onto Fleet Street and take the first right onto Trafalgar Arches. Follow the lane as it turns left, with the arches that support platform 8 of Brighton Station looming to your right.

8 Cross Trafalgar Street at the zebra crossing and turn left down the hill. After the first side street, take the next alleyway on your right, Trafalgar Terrace. Note the unusual arrangement: the cottages on your right have 'detached' gardens on the opposite side of the alley. At the end, turn right then immediately left in front of the pub into Frederick Gardens. When you emerge onto North Road turn left and take the fourth right turn – the narrow Orange Row – and follow it round as it turns to the right.

9 At the end of Orange Row turn left, then at Church Street cross over and take the side street ahead of you, slightly to the left: Jew Street. As Jew Street widens into a car park, turn left down a twitten. About halfway down on the right, note the filled-in brick archway ★ – this has been suggested as the possible entrance to Brighton's earliest synagogue, dating from around 1790. Turn right onto Bond Street and at the end turn right onto North Street. Cross at the pedestrian lights and turn along Ship Street to find yourself back at the start.

AZ walk five

Quirky Kemptown

The LGBTQ+ quarter, an urban village and the beach.

This is a colourful and varied walk exploring the secret delights of the east side of the city. In the first part of the walk we visit St James's Street, the centre of LGBTQ+ life in Brighton since the 1980s, with its lively mix of shops, cafés and nightlife.

We continue east through a variety of seaside architecture – including Brighton's first sea-facing crescent and an Indian-inspired mausoleum – and into Kemptown, one of Brighton's most colourful urban villages, centred on St George's Road. Here, away from the tourist crowds, there is an interesting selection of independent local businesses, a hint of eccentricity, and you may possibly bump into a celebrity or two…

The walk climaxes with the grandest of all seafront set pieces: Sussex Square and Lewes Crescent. This forms the core of the original Kemp Town, developed in the 1820s by Thomas Read Kemp, landowner and MP, to provide London-quality housing for Brighton's wealthiest visitors.

We then head back along the eastern stretch of beach where we enjoy long sea views and take in some easily missed features, including a hidden tunnel, a ride in a Victorian lift and an unofficial beach sculpture garden.

start / finish	Brighton Palace Pier, Madeira Drive
nearest postcode	BN2 1TW
distance	3¼ miles / 5.3 km
time	1 hour 30 minutes
terrain	Paved roads, some steps, pebble beach (optional).

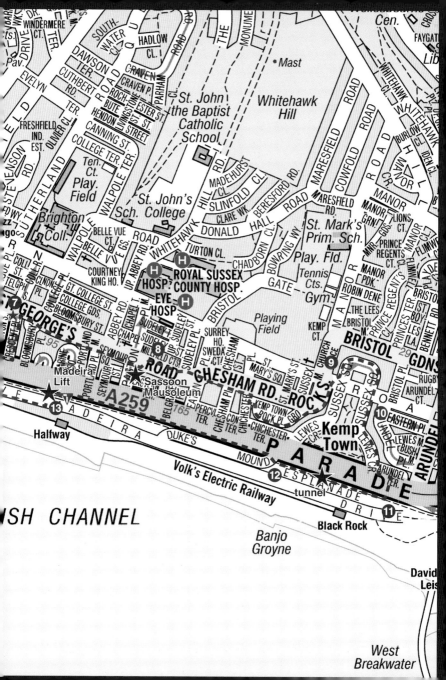

WINDERMERE CT.

SOUTH-

WATER
CL.

HADLOW
CL.

ROAD

THE

MONUME

• Mast

FAYGATE

Lib

Pav.

EVELYN

DAWSON
TER.

CUTHBERT
RD.

CRAVEN
TER.

CRAVEN P.

ROCHESTER ST.

LIVINGSTONE ST.

PARHAM

St. John
the Baptist
Catholic
School

Whitehawk
Hill

WHITEHAWK
CL.

WHITEHAWK
HILL

IDEN

BURLON
CL.

FRESHFIELD
IND.
EST.

BUTE ST.

HENDON
STREET

CANNING ST.

COLLEGE TER.

WALPOLE TER.

Ten.
Ct.
Play.
Field

St. John's
Sch. College

ROAD

HILL RD.

MADEHURST
CL.

SLINFOLD
CL.

BERESFORD RD.

CLARE WK.

DONALD

HALL

MARESFIELD

ROAD

ROAD

COWFOLD

ROAD

MANOR
GRN.

LIONS
CT.

MANOR

MANOR

PRINCE
REGENTS

FLINWE

STENVENSON
RD.

SUTHERLAND

Brighton
Coll.

BELLE VUE
CT.

BELLE VUE GS.

WHITEHAWK ROAD

TURTON CL.

CHADBORN CL.

BOWRING WY.

MARESFIELD
RD.

St. Mark's
Prim. Sch.

Play. Fld.

MANOR
PDK.

ROBIN DENE

PRINCE REGENTS

MANOR

BRISTO

COURTNEY
KING HO.

UP. ABBEY RD.

ABBEY RD.

H

HOSP.

ROYAL SUSSEX
COUNTY HOSP.

EYE
HOSP

H

BRISTOL

Tennis
Cts.

GATE

Play. Fld.

Gym.

THE LEES

BRISTOL
M.

KEMP
CT.

BRISTOL

GDNS

7

GEORGE'S

COLLI

GT. COLLEGE ST.

COLLEGE GDS.

BLOOMSBURY ST.

CLNDN.

PL.

BLOOMSBURY
PL. 95

PORTLAND

CHAPEL T.

SUDELEY

UP. SUDELEY ST.

ST.

SUDELEY PL.

Surrey
HO.

SWEDA
CT.

ST. MARY'S SQ.

ST.
MARY'S ST.

CHESHAM
ST.

SUSSEX
M.

CHURCH

RUGBY

ARUNDEL
CT.

Madeira
Lift

8

MILE END
COTTS.

ROAD

CHESHAM RD.

ROCKS

SUSSEX SQ.

SUSSEX SQ.

9

Sassoon
Mausoleum

A259

765

PORTLAND PL.

SEYMOUR
SQ.

BELGRAVE
PL.

EASTERN
PL.

PERCIVAL
TER.

CHESHAM
TER.

CHICHESTER
TER.

CON.
TER.

KEMP TOWN
ROCK PL. GRO.

CHICHESTER
TER.

LEWES CR.

Kemp
Town

SUSSEX

LEWES CR.

10

EASTERN PL.

ARUNDEL

Halfway

13

MADEIRA

DUKE'S

MOUND

LEWES
M.

BUSH
PL.M.

ARUNDEL
TER.

PARADE

Volk's Electric Railway

ESPLANADE

tunnel

12

DRIVE

11

SH CHANNEL

Black Rock

Banjo
Groyne

West
Breakwater

David
Leis

① Facing the entrance of Brighton Palace Pier ★ , take the steps to the left down to the beach. After a few metres enter the tunnel towards SEA LIFE Brighton. At the time of writing, the tunnel has murals depicting music stars with connections to the city. (If the tunnel is closed, return to the upper promenade and cross to the SEA LIFE entrance.)

② You emerge in the forecourt of SEA LIFE Brighton ★ . Opened in 1872, it is the world's oldest operating aquarium. Walk up the steps and turn right onto Marine Parade. Cross at the pedestrian lights to the north side. Turn right, then take the second left into Charles Street. This is one of the oldest surviving residential streets in Brighton (1780s) with local black mathematical tiles and tightly curved bow windows.

③ At the end, cross St James's Street and turn left. Look for a narrow passage about 55 yards (50 metres) down on your right – St James's Place ★ . Behind the locked gate is a surprising row of well-kept cottages. Retrace your steps to head up St James's Street. This is where Brighton's title of 'LGBTQ+ capital of Britain' is most visible, busy with cafés, shops and pubs.

④ At the corner of Madeira Place on the right, look at the plaque saying that this was the first pub 'to discover a taste for Tuaca in 1996'. Tuaca is an Italian liqueur which has become an iconic Brighton drink – it's popular across the city, but almost unheard of elsewhere. Continue up St James's Street – feel free to explore the interesting side streets – until it opens out to a sea-facing square, New Steine.

⑤ In the gardens, note the sculpture: Brighton and Hove AIDS Memorial which, at the time of writing, is one of only two in the country commemorating those affected by the disease which has killed an estimated 40 million people worldwide. Continue past St Mary's ★ , another of Brighton's impressive Victorian churches. After about 275 yards (250 metres), at the traffic lights, turn right down Bedford Street.

⑥ At the seafront road, turn left, then after a short while turn into Royal Crescent, the city's first sea-facing architectural composition (1800). Note the black mathematical tiles, the first-floor verandas and number 4, former house of actor Laurence Olivier. Continue east along the seafront road. After you pass Burlington Street, take the next left towards the narrow Crescent Place.

7 At the end turn right onto St George's Road, the heart of Kemptown village. After about 330 yards (300 metres) you pass St George's Church, built for the residents of Sussex Square and Lewes Crescent. Today you can visit the café, enjoy the gardens or attend a concert. On the next right-hand corner is the Sassoon Mausoleum ★, now a cabaret club, built for the family of businessman Albert Sassoon who lived nearby, and whose Indian connections are reflected in the architecture.

8 Continue on the left-hand side of the road and at the end cross Eaton Place to continue straight ahead along Chesham Road. Take the second right into Chichester Place, then left into Kemp Town Place. Note the private residential road ahead of you with its black and white cobbled coach houses. Follow the road as it goes right then left behind the coach houses. When you join Rock Street continue ahead on the right-hand pavement.

9 At the busy Eastern Road, cross at the zebra crossing and turn right. Turn left into Sussex Square, centrepiece of the Kemp Town estate. Note the plaque on the first house to *Alice's Adventures in Wonderland* author Lewis Carroll, who regularly visited his sister here. On the top side of the square, number 22 was the home of Thomas Kemp, creator of Kemp Town.

10 On the third side of the square continue down towards the sea as it becomes Lewes Crescent. Note on your right the extensive landscaped gardens of Kemp Town Enclosures, accessible only to keyholding residents. When you reach the seafront road, turn left, cross the road at the pedestrian lights, turn right and then almost immediately go left down the steps.

11 At the bottom of the steps, turn right along the gravel esplanade. Looking towards the beach, note the station of Volk's Railway, the world's oldest operating electric railway (1883). (You could optionally take this train back to the pier.) Shortly on the right, note the white buildings set in the wall, either side of a gated tunnel ★, with a glimpse of the Kemp Town Enclosures beyond. This is a private tunnel for the residents of Lewes Crescent to access the beach.

12 At the end of the esplanade, take the path uphill to join the road. Turn right, then immediately take the pedestrian crossing left to continue along the upper promenade of Marine Parade. Walk for about ⅓ mile (650 metres) (passing Paston Place, the start for walk eleven). On the left, opposite Marine Square, you will see the fish-themed entrance pavilion to the Madeira Lift ★ (1890).

13 If the lift is open (usually Easter to September), press the call button. It is operated by an attendant so it might take a few minutes to arrive. You exit unexpectedly into a former Victorian tearoom, now a nightclub, and you pass the stage where acts including Kaiser Chiefs and Ed Sheeran have played. (If the lift is not in operation, walk further along the promenade and take the next set of steps down.) Continue in the direction of the pier on the beach side of the road. Note the impressive 19th-century Madeira Terraces, stretching over ½ mile (800 metres).

14 After about ¼ mile (400 metres), look for the fenced off enclosure on the beach on the other side of the railway line. Cross the line at the next crossing then walk left across the pebbles to the Flint Grotto ★, an 'unofficial' sculpture garden of fantastical figures, created by a Brighton fisherman on a patch of beach traditionally used for storage. Return to the promenade and continue past the statue of Brighton-born athlete Steve Ovett, gold medal-winner in the 1980 Olympics, and the Volk's Railway station (you can visit the free exhibition), then return to the pier.

AZ walk six

Squares, Terraces and Gardens

Regency and Victorian conservation areas.

This is a fun and varied walk which starts right in the busy centre of Brighton, yet within a few minutes you can escape to the medieval St Nicholas' Church, with its hidden garden in an almost village atmosphere. We then explore the interconnected areas of Clifton Hill and Montpelier, which have some of the city's most attractive white and cream villas – again, it's hard to believe we are just a block or two away from the commercial city centre. Powis Square in particular is a delightful hidden gem.

We then make our way to St Ann's Well Gardens, where Dr Richard Russell (see walk one) sent his patients to drink the iron-rich water as a supplement to his seawater cures. In the 19th century it was developed as a pleasure garden complete with hermit's cave and hot air balloon. There is then another hidden garden in the grounds of a meditation centre.

Some of Brighton's most original architecture can be enjoyed on this walk, including an Indian-inspired house, an old French church and three gorgeous, interconnected squares that conclude our walk. Along the way, we follow in the footsteps of some prominent residents, including Winston Churchill, who was sent to school here at the age of 9, painter John Constable who came to Brighton with his wife to aid her recovery from tuberculosis, and poet Lord Alfred 'Bosie' Douglas.

start / finish	Churchill Square shopping centre (by Western Road)
nearest postcode	BN1 2TA
distance	3 miles / 4.8 km
time	1 hour 15 minutes
terrain	Paved road and paths, steps and gentle hills.

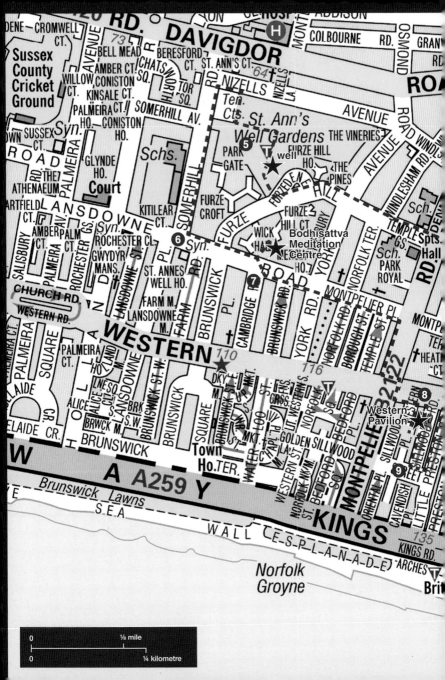

1 Facing Western Road with the shopping centre behind you, walk right, towards the traffic lights. Cross to the left at the lights, then immediately turn right to cross again. Turn left so that you are heading uphill along Dyke Road. Keep right and take the path that soon forks off towards a churchyard. On the right note the castellations and turrets of Wykeham Terrace, a rare example of early 19th-century Regency Gothic architecture.

2 Walk up towards the church. Note the grave just to the right of the path, surrounded by a small fence: Phoebe Hessel dressed as a man to fight in the army and lived to the age of 108. The 14th-century St Nicholas' Church ★ was Brighton's original parish church and is well worth a visit. Turn left in front of the church, which brings you to a road. Turn left, then at the road junction cross and go through the arched gateway ahead of you.

3 You are now in St Nicholas' Rest Garden ★ , a former cemetery and now a secluded city retreat. Follow the path in either direction around the garden and exit the way you came. Turn left then left again and up the steps to walk along the pavement of Clifton Terrace. You are entering a conservation area with some of the best examples of Regency-style villas. At the end turn right, then take the second left into Powis Square.

4 At the bottom of the square turn left then right into Victoria Road. St Michael's Church ★ is Grade I listed and has decorations and stained glass by leading Victorian artists William Morris and Edward Burne-Jones. Continue along this road for about 330 yards (300 metres). It becomes Furze Hill. Near the bottom of the hill, turn right into St Ann's Well Gardens. Take the left-hand surfaced path, and when you reach another fork, keep left. On your right note the site of the original well ★ , a reminder of the park's history as a health spa.

5 Continue past the café on your left and turn left past the café entrance. Just before the tennis courts, take the path to the right. Continue to the road (ignore the path turning right). At Nizells Avenue, note the block of flats ahead and a plaque to the lover of Oscar Wilde, Lord Alfred Douglas, who coined the phrase 'the love that dare not speak its name'. Turn left and left again onto Somerhill Road.

6 At the end, turn left onto Lansdowne Road. After about 220 yards (200 metres), look for the gates on the left leading to the driveway of the Bodhisattva Meditation Centre ★ . Usually, the garden is open to quiet visitors (check the sign by the gate for opening times) – if open, walk down the drive and the garden is on the right just before the main house. Turn back to continue along Lansdowne Road, and cross to the right-hand pavement.

7 On the corner of the next junction on your right, note the plaque to the former prep school once attended by Winston Churchill. Continue on the same road for nearly 400 yards (350 metres). At the traffic light junction, turn right onto Montpelier Road. At the next crossroads turn left, use the lights to cross to the diagonally opposite corner. Turn right so that you are walking on the right-hand pavement of Western Road.

8 Take the first right to view the Western Pavilion ★ , a homage to the Indian-inspired Royal Pavilion, built by Regency architect Amon H. Wilds as his own home. He also designed the gothic building opposite and the terrace a bit further down (note the pun on his name Amon – ammonite fossils – at the top of the columns). Head back to Western Road, turn right then take the first right down Sillwood Road. At number 11 on your left, artist John Constable stayed – about 150 of his works were inspired by his visits to Brighton.

9 At the end of the road turn left then left again. When you return to Western Road, turn right then take the first right into Preston Street, lined with restaurants. Take the fourth turning on the left into Regency Square (also probably by A. H. Wilds). Walk ahead to the far side and turn towards the sea on the left-hand side of the square. Here you have a grand view of the 530-foot (162-metre) high Brighton i360 ★ observation tower and the remains of the West Pier, destroyed by fire in 2003.

10 Before you reach the seafront road, turn left into Queensbury Mews. Here you can see a former French Protestant church ★ , now a private residence, opposite what is believed to be the smallest pub in Brighton, both in the shadow of the enormous Metropole Hotel. Turn left at the church.

11 At the top, turn right and walk through the passageway next to the pub, which takes you into Russell Square. Turn left and follow the square round to the right to take the left turn up the hill into Clarence Square. Head for the top right corner and turn right. Continue ahead and you emerge onto Churchill Square to return to the start.

AZ walk seven

Discovering London Road

History with a modern urban edge.

Many visitors have seen the London Road area through their car window as they sit in traffic on their way to the beach or the Lanes. Dominated by busy roads and a long way from the sea, this is certainly the most 'urban' of the walks in this book and might not seem an obvious destination at first glance. But, as one of the earliest of Brighton's suburbs, this is an area that is steeped in history and interest, and its recent regeneration and influx of students have given London Road a new air of edgy urban creativity.

We will see some of the city's best examples of early 19th-century housing, and two stunning Victorian churches: St Peter's by Charles Barry – architect of the Houses of Parliament – and St Bartholomew's, 'the tallest parish church in Europe'. For shopping and eating, London Road and the Open Market offer some of the most interesting and good-value outlets, including a fish and chip shop which doubles as a museum to Brighton's most famous comedian, Max Miller.

We can also enjoy the leisure and cultural attractions of the area, including one of the country's oldest cinemas, one of Brighton's most popular parks, and a community art gallery.

start / finish	South side of St Peter's Church, between St George's Place and Richmond Place
nearest postcode	BN1 4GB
distance	2 miles / 3.3 km
time	1 hour
terrain	Paved roads and paths, no steep hills.

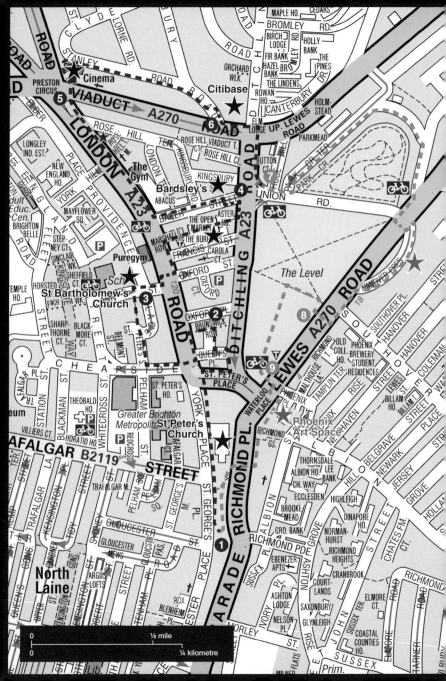

1 Start by facing the tower of St Peter's Church ★ then walking along the pavement to the left of the church. Pass the church, continue ahead and cross the road at the pedestrian lights, then turn right along St Peter's Place. Turn left and immediately left again into Queen's Place. Turn right and walk past the black and white tarred cobble cottages, built around 1815.

2 At the end, turn left down the alleyway to reach the main London Road and turn left. Cross the main road at the pedestrian crossing and turn the corner to head up Cheapside. Take the first turning on the right, St Peter's Street, and you can see the colossal height of St Bartholomew's Church ★ ahead of you (the nave roof is higher than Westminster Abbey's). If it is open, go in to experience the vast uninterrupted space and the elaborate high altar.

3 Looking at the church, turn right down the hill and at London Road, turn left then cross to the other side and walk along the right-hand pavement for about 110 yards (100 metres). Turn right into Marshalls Row which leads into the Open Market ★ , with a variety of independent food and retail choices. When you exit the market at the far end, turn left.

4 Take the next left down Baker Street, and almost immediately on the right-hand side is Bardsley's ★ , which has been selling fish and chips since 1926 and also contains a small museum dedicated to Brighton entertainer Max Miller. At the end of the street, turn right down London Road, keeping to the right-hand side.

5 After about 275 yards (250 metres), you come to large road junction. Go straight over and after the fire station is the Duke of York's Picturehouse ★ , which has been showing films since 1910 and is the oldest unaltered cinema in the country. Note the burlesque legs above the balcony. Turn right after the cinema and walk the whole length of Stanley Road, which becomes Shaftesbury Road near the end.

6 At the end of Shaftesbury Road turn left, noting the elaborate flint building on your left, Citibase Brighton ★ , built in 1854 as a teacher training college, now offices. At the main crossroads, use the pedestrian lights to cross to the opposite corner, so that you are walking downhill on the left-hand side of Ditchling Road.

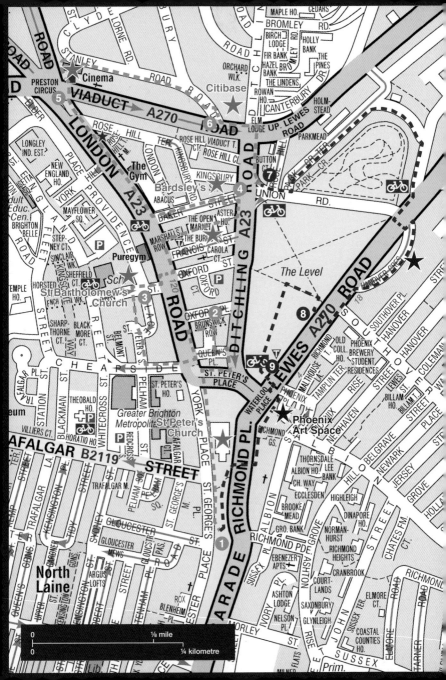

7 Take the next left onto Union Road, then the second left onto Park Crescent Terrace. Keep right so that you walk all the way round the crescent. At the busy Lewes Road, turn right and then go straight across the pedestrian lights, then turn left to cross Lewes Road at another set of lights. On the other side of Lewes Road turn left then immediately right into Hanover Crescent ★ with its wonderful set of Georgian houses. Returning to Lewes Road at the far end of the crescent, turn left and cross at the pedestrian lights towards the park known as The Level.

8 On the other side of the road bear slightly right to the path that takes you into the park then take the left fork along a surfaced path. About halfway along the path, turn left through the water feature garden. Continue ahead through the gates of the playground and exit The Level.

9 Turn left and cross the large junction ahead of you. On the other side, turn right past the entrance to Phoenix Art Space ★ gallery – often open for exhibitions. Continue along the main road and cross at the pedestrian lights to take you back to St Peter's Church.

AZ walk eight

An Elegant Georgian Estate

The peculiar charm of Brunswick Town.

Brunswick Town, just on the Hove side of the city centre, is Brighton and Hove at its best: two stunning squares, a crescent, grand Regency architecture, and side streets bursting with character and history.

Created in the 1820s by Brighton architect Charles Busby as an answer to Kemp Town at the eastern end of town, it was planned as a self-contained residential estate incorporating housing, stabling, a market hall, church and pubs. The class system was built into the plan with palatial facades fronting the best houses on Brunswick Square, middle-class housing on the side streets, and, tucked in behind, mews streets for the horses and domestic staff.

Today most of the grand town houses have been divided into flats, the old stables have been elevated to desirable human abodes, and the market hall is now a hub of creative arts. And it's this mixture of planning and modern reinterpretation that makes the area so enjoyable – a variety of well-kept white and cream stuccoed houses, hidden side streets with cottages, pubs, small businesses and a community garden.

The walk continues west to the mid-1800s Palmeira Square, which merges onto the majestic sweeping curves of Adelaide Crescent before returning past some of the best seafront architecture in the city.

start / finish	Brighton Bandstand on Kings Road
nearest postcode	BN1 2PQ
distance	2¼ miles / 3.5 km
time	1 hour
terrain	Paved road and paths, short cobbled section, some steps (optional), no hills.

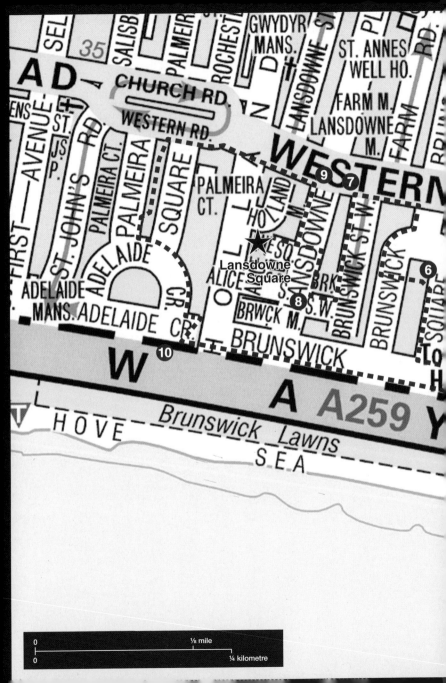

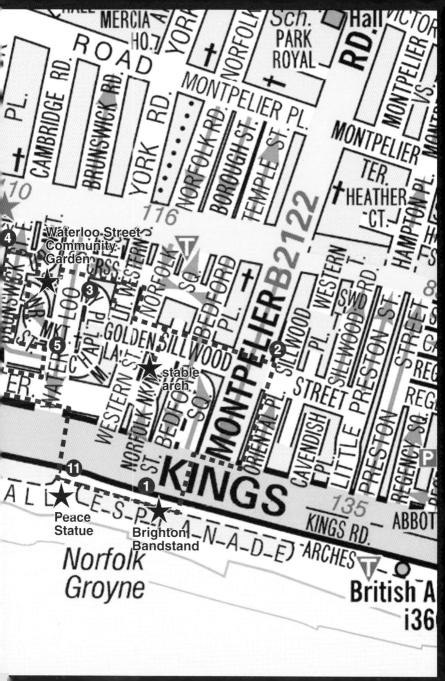

1 Start by Brighton Bandstand ★, a fine example of a Victorian bandstand. Cross the road at the pedestrian lights, turn right and shortly take the second left into Oriental Place. Note the scallop shell designs above the windows and the columns topped with spirals inspired by ammonite fossils – a pun on the name of the architect Amon H. Wilds (see also walk six).

2 Turn left onto Sillwood Street. After two crossroads, look left down Norfolk Buildings – note the arch entrance to a former stable ★ with a horse head sculpture and the flint coach house on the bottom right. Return to continue along Sillwood Street and at the end, turn right up to Norfolk Square, then take the first left into Norfolk Place.

3 At the end of the street, head across the road and left for a short distance, to find the arched entrance to the Waterloo Street Community Garden ★ . By the entrance is the weathered headless statue of Captain William Pechell, son of a Brighton MP, who died in the Crimean War. Walk through the garden and turn right and follow the path round to the front of The Old Market – built in the 1820s as a market hall, it is now an arts centre where the worldwide hit show *Stomp* was first developed.

4 Keeping The Old Market to your left, turn left and left again, then right after the pub down Lower Market Street. At the bottom just before the corner, take the passage to your right to cut through to Brunswick Street East, then turn left. Follow it round to the end and emerge onto Waterloo Street – note St Andrew's Church ahead of you, the first church in England built in the Italianate style, and the work of Charles Barry, who went on to design the Houses of Parliament.

5 Turn right and right again on the seafront road. Take the next right into Brunswick Square, the heart of the Brunswick Town development. Walk about two-thirds of the way up. Number 13, The Regency Town House, is being restored as a heritage project and is open occasionally for art exhibitions and pre-booked guided tours. Continue a short way up and cross the road to the gate and enter the gardens.

6 Walk across the restored Regency gardens and through the gate on the opposite side of the square. Number 45 has a plaque to the childhood home of Edward Carpenter, 19th-century social reformer and early gay rights activist. Turn right towards the top of the square and turn left onto Brunswick Place up to the busy Western Road, where you turn left again.

7 On the next corner on the left, note The Freemasons tavern with its elaborate 1920s Art Deco frontage. Turn left here down Brunswick Street West, originally lined with stables serving the houses of Brunswick Square behind. Further down on the right, the modern building is BIMM (originally Brighton Institute of Modern Music), where musicians including James Bay and Tom Odell have studied their trade. Take the next right.

8 Turn right onto Lansdowne Place and at the first house note the home of Charles Busby, architect of Brunswick town. Cross over and take a brief diversion to admire the Busby buildings in Lansdowne Square ★ (more of a side street than a square), then continue to walk up Lansdowne Place, with its beautiful villas along the left-hand side. Also note on the right the plaque to John Leech, the first illustrator of Charles Dickens' original *A Christmas Carol.*

9 At the main Western Road, turn left. Beyond the traffic lights the road opens out to the elegant Palmeira Square. Continue to the bus stop, where you take the path left into the garden. Take the right-hand fork to follow the west (right) side of the garden. At the end, take the slope on the right up to the road, as the square now becomes Adelaide Crescent. Turn left to follow the east side of the crescent as it curves towards the sea.

10 At the end of the crescent, turn left and take the steps down to the seafront road. (From here you could explore further into Hove by joining walk twelve). To avoid the steps, follow the road to the right around the open end of the crescent as far as the first stone pillar. Turn left and follow the seafront road for about a third of a mile (600 metres). After you pass the end of Waterloo Street, cross at the pedestrian lights to the Peace Statue ★ , topped with an angel. This is a memorial to King Edward VII and stands on the border between Hove and Brighton, which were separate towns until 1997.

11 Look back across the road to the large block of flats, Embassy Court. Built in the 1930s in sleek modernist style, this was once the most glamorous address in Brighton and home to stars including playwright Terence Rattigan. From here, continue along the promenade to finish the walk at the bandstand.

AZ walk nine

Three Hills Challenge

An adventure around the suburbs.

Over three hills and three parks, this is an urban ramble that takes a broad swathe through the best of suburban Brighton. With hills come views – you will be treated to surprise glimpses of the sea, the countryside and the city – and *cat creeps*: alleyways with long flights of steps. Dyke Road Park contains Brighton Open Air Theatre, opposite the Victorian curiosities of the Booth Museum of Natural History.

Preston Park has a magical rock garden, a medieval village church, Preston Manor (open seasonally as a museum) and a hidden pet graveyard. You can also see many elm trees – after disease destroyed most of Britain's elms, Brighton retains the largest collection in the country.

Amongst the residential suburbs, we pass through the hillside district of Hanover, affectionately known as 'muesli mountain' due to its alternative and eco-conscious image, with its colourful painted houses and friendly local pubs. Queen's Park, set in the bowl valley of a former villa, is perhaps the city's most romantic park, with the Pepper Pot tower and former spa buildings of the German Spa, a reminder of Brighton's days as a health resort.

With so much to enjoy and explore, it is recommended that you allow the best part of a day for this walk, and savour the many opportunities for rest and refreshment along the way.

start / finish	Brighton Railway Station, Queen's Road
nearest postcode	BN1 3XE
distance	6¼ miles / 10 km
time	3 hours 30 minutes
terrain	Paved roads and paths, some long steep hills, steps, some uneven paving stones (optional) and stepping stones across a small pond (optional).

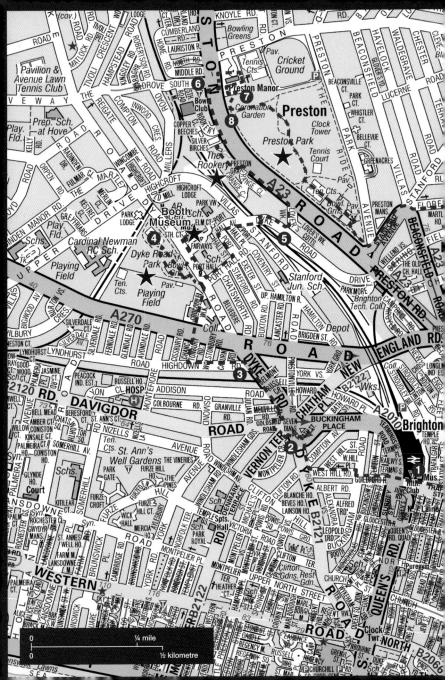

❶ Starting with Brighton Station behind you, go right across the lights and ahead up Guildford Road. At the top, turn right and immediately left up West Hill Road. At the end turn right down Dyke Road.

❷ Just before the roundabout, turn left across the zebra crossing, then over the next zebra crossing at Vernon Terrace. Then turn right and follow the pavement as it goes round to the left. Cross a third zebra crossing to reach the other side of Goldsmid Road. Turn right and follow this pavement as it goes left and rejoins Dyke Road.

❸ After about 330 yards (300 metres), turn left onto Highdown Road. Take the third right up Chanctonbury Road. Continue ahead over the zebra crossing and up an alleyway. At the end turn left onto Dyke Road then immediately take the first path left into Dyke Road Park ★. After the playground, turn left, then the next right, then left. Through the fence, you can see Brighton Open Air Theatre.

❹ After the theatre, follow the path right and take a sharp right across the formal garden. After the garden, turn left to the main road and the pedestrian lights. After crossing Dyke Road, turn left and shortly you come to Booth Museum ★. Retrace your steps down Dyke Road and after about 220 yards (200 metres), turn left into Port Hall Road. Then after about 165 yards (150 metres), turn left down Port Hall Street and continue as

it swings right. Halfway over the railway bridge, cross to the left side.

❺ Soon after the bridge, look for a gap in the wall on your left, leading down a flight of steps. At the bottom, continue down the small road and turn left onto Preston Road. After the turning for Grange Close, on your left is the Rock Garden ★. Take the main path through the garden, taking care over the uneven rocks and stepping stones. (Alternatively, continue along the pavement.) Exit the garden at the far end and turn left along Preston Road to the traffic lights.

❻ Cross Preston Road at the lights and continue. Shortly before the next junction, go through the gate on your right (if closed: continue ahead, turn right then right again), which takes you to Preston Manor. Take the path to the left of the house, up some steps and through an arch. Turn left through another arch to St Peter's Church, which is often open to visitors. Exiting the church, go back down the steps, but this time follow the path left onto the lawn of Preston Manor.

❼ Head for the arch on the other side of the lawn, down some steps into the walled garden. Turn right and walk anticlockwise round the garden. Approaching the third (southwest) corner, along the wall, note the pet graves belonging to the former owners of Preston Manor. After the headstones, turn right through the gate into Preston Park ★. Beside the path, on the right, is a large hollow Elm tree, one of the Preston Twins, thought to be the oldest English Elm anywhere (1613). Opposite, the trunk of its late twin has been preserved as a sculpture.

8 At the wide drive, turn left. Then take the path to the right, taking you past the café and across the middle of Preston Park. At the far end, take the path that goes between the tennis courts. Continue into the Rose Garden. Bear right and head for the exit at the far end. Out of the park, turn left up Stanford Avenue. As the road begins to climb at the traffic fork, turn right across the island and head up Florence Road.

9 At the top, cross the road at the lights and turn right along Ditchling Road. After the garage, turn left up Prince's Road, then right onto Crescent Road. At the end, cross over and turn left. At the junction, go straight ahead to find a gap between the houses which takes you down the long flight of steps. At the bottom turn right, then carefully cross the busy road and continue ahead down St Paul's Street. At the end, turn left onto Lewes Road and cross at the lights, then turn left.

10 Turn right up Franklin Road. Take the second right onto De Montfort Road. At the end, carefully cross to continue ahead along Hampden Road and into the colourful neighbourhood of Hanover. At the end, turn left up Islingword Road. At the top, cross Queen's Park Road using the lights on your left and turn right to find the

Pepper Pot tower ★. Built in the grounds of a villa that once stood nearby, its purpose is unknown. Bear left behind the Pepper Pot down Tower Road.

11 At the end, continue ahead and enter Queen's Park ★. Follow this footpath as it bears right, then take the left fork down the hill. At a junction of paths go through the second (left-hand) gate, then take the next right to continue downhill, then take the right fork past the lake. At the bottom of the lake, turn left through the gate and immediately turn right up the hill. Note the columns of the former German Spa (1835) on the left.

12 At the top of the path, turn right and after about 165 yards (150 metres), turn left uphill and out of the park. Cross over and walk up Albion Hill. Cross the busy road to continue along Albion Hill and take the second right down Montreal Road. At the mini-roundabout take the second exit and head all the way down Southover Street.

13 At the bottom, turn left, cross at the lights and turn left. Continue ahead over the next crossing and bear right to take you to the right of St Peter's Church (walk seven starts near here). Cross over to walk down the right-hand pavement then turn right up Trafalgar Street. Continue to the top of the street, passing the Toy and Model Museum under the bridge, then turn sharp right at the top to return to Brighton Station.

ᴀᴢ walk ten

Cemetery Walk

A haven of peace and sepulchral beauty.

A few steps away from the noise and traffic of Lewes Road lies another world: a cluster of Victorian municipal cemeteries in a wooded valley, where elaborate tombs and gothic chapels compete with trees, shrubs and wildlife. Some parts of this walk are so wild that it feels like a countryside walk – you may barely meet another living soul – while in other places it is more of a sculpture park dedicated to 19th-century lives and the mourning of them.

We explore two interconnected burial grounds. The Extra Mural Cemetery was established in 1851 as a privately run burial ground in response both to new public health laws and Brighton's increasing popularity as an affluent residential town. This was the peak of fashion for elaborate grave monuments and mausoleums – indeed the cemetery was regarded as a tourist attraction as early as the 1880s. After falling into disuse in the 1950s, the town council acquired it as a memorial ground. Some sculptures have been restored; elsewhere, nature has been allowed to take over as crumbling gravestones are engulfed with roots and ivy.

The adjoining Woodvale Cemetery was built around the same time as the Extra Mural and a crematorium was added in the 1930s. Still very much in use (singer Dame Vera Lynn was cremated here in 2020), Woodvale has some well-tended garden areas, but also large parts where nature has the upper hand.

There is a regular bus service between the city centre and the crematorium.

start / finish	Entrance to Woodvale Crematorium, Lewes Road
nearest postcode	BN2 3QB
distance	1½ miles / 2.5 km
time	1 hour
terrain	Surfaced roads and paths. Gravel, grass and dirt paths, steps and some short, steep hills.

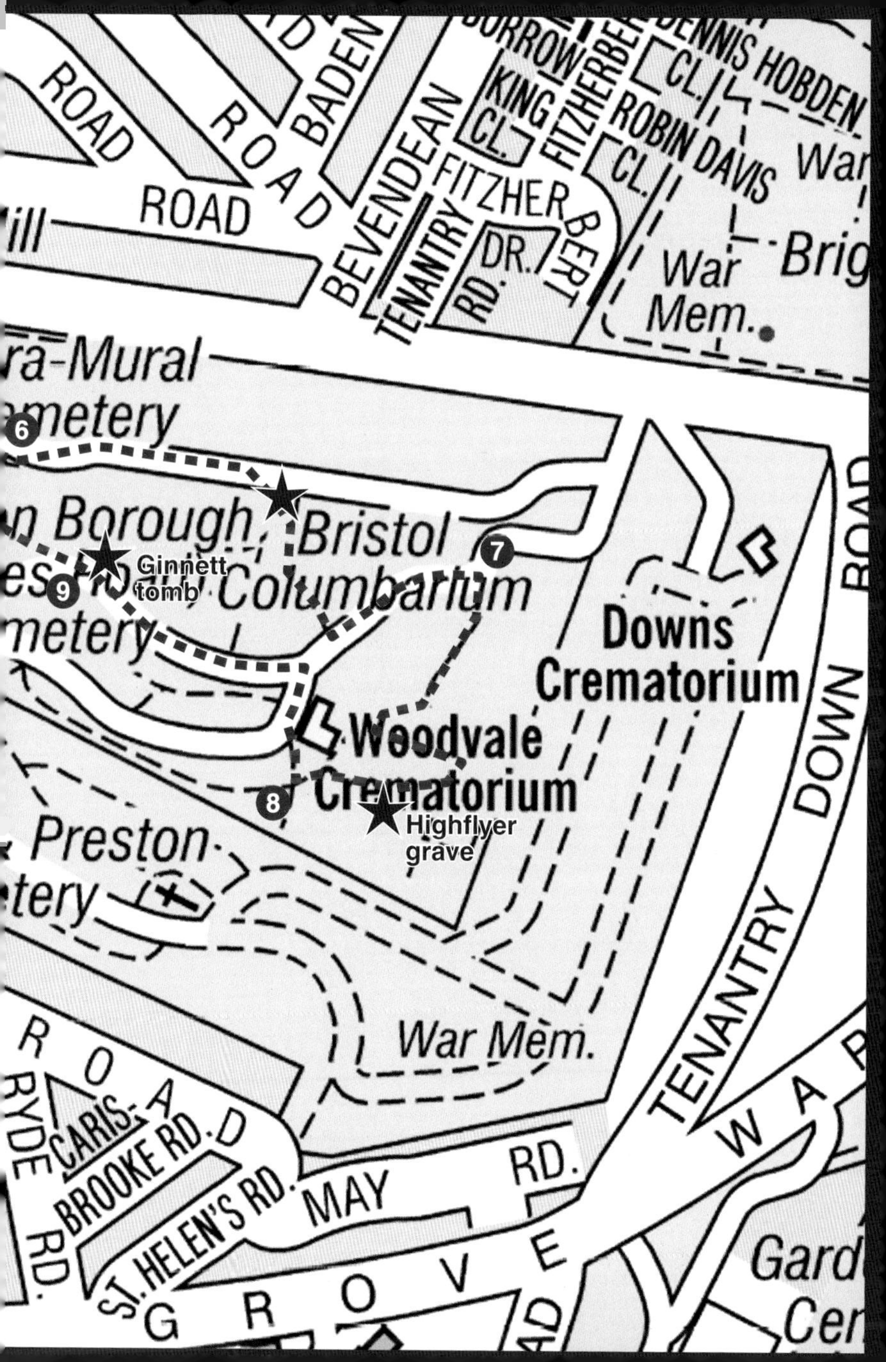

ROAD

ROAD

ROAD

BADEN

BEVENDEAN

FITZHER BERT

TENANTRY RD.

DR.

KING CL.

BURROW

FITZHERBE

ROBIN DAVIS

CL.

CL.

DENNIS HOBDEN

War

Brig

War Mem.

ra-Mural
metery

Borough
es
metery

Bristol
Columbarium

Ginnett
tomb

Downs
Crematorium

ROAD

Woodvale
Crematorium

Highflyer
grave

Preston
tery

DOWN

War Mem.

TENANTRY

CARIS-
BROOKE RD.

A
D

RYDE RD.

ST. HELEN'S RD.

MAY

GROVE

RD.

RD.

WAR

Gard
Cen

1 Start at the entrance (signposted 'Woodvale Crematorium') and walk up the driveway. When you pass the flint Woodvale Lodge, look on your left for some steps signposted 'Pedestrian entrance to the Extra Mural Cemetery'. Go up the steps then keep left to follow the path down the hill.

2 When you reach the road, turn right. Here, and for much of the remainder of the walk, you can see Victorian grave monuments, including angels, urns, broken columns, Celtic crosses and obelisks. Ahead is the flint Extra Mural Chapel designed by A. H. Wilds, architect of much of Regency Brighton. Just past the chapel is a square flint building, which almost looks part of the chapel but is in fact the largest mausoleum in the cemetery, belonging to the Ray family ★ .

3 Turn round and walk so that the chapel is on your right. Turn right after the chapel, taking the grass path up the hill. After a few steps, take the path right, indicated by an arrow, and follow the stepped path up the hill. Here the gravestones have been almost entirely absorbed into the woodland. At the next junction, turn right, still following the arrow waymark, onto a wider grassy track.

4 Shortly, in the centre of the path, is the outsize tomb of John Rastrick ★ , an engineer responsible for the London to Brighton railway – his tomb represents a railway turntable. Continue ahead and, at the end of the path, turn right down the hill. At the road, turn right. Ignore the first path that goes off to the left, and enjoy the well-preserved gravestones and the catacombs set into the wall on the right.

5 Further down the hill take the second (grass) path on the left – it's opposite a single obelisk to the Sampson family. Almost immediately you come to Gerard Ford's impressive mausoleum ★ , surrounded by a decorative wrought iron fence. Turn left here, and follow the woodland path up the hill.

6 When you rejoin the road, continue ahead up the hill and the woodland soon opens out to a Garden of Remembrance. This is currently in use, so please be respectful of mourners. The flint building on your right is a columbarium ★ built to house cremated remains. Turn right in front of this building and follow the main path all the way down the hill. You are now in Woodvale Cemetery. At the road, turn left and follow the road as it curves right.

7 At the sharp left bend, turn right onto a wide grass path. Follow this path as it eventually zig-zags down the hill and at the bottom of the steps turn left up a gravel track. At the next junction note the sign for Thomas Highflyer's grave, turn right and keep right up the grassy path. In the woodland opposite a bench you can see the simple white cross to Thomas Highflyer ★, who was born in East Africa and rescued by a British anti-slavery patrol. He died in Brighton in 1870, aged 12.

8 Continue until the path crosses some steps. Take the steps down to your right to reach the Woodvale Crematorium Chapels, two interconnected buildings from the 1850s. Be mindful of any funerals taking place and walk past the front of the chapels. After you pass the end of the North Chapel, at the road junction turn left down the hill.

9 After about 110 yards (100 metres), note the large tomb topped with a circus pony, created for John Frederick Ginnett ★ and his family of circus managers and performers. Here, take the grass path that leaves the road to the right. At the end turn left, then right through the collapsed wall to take you back into the Extra Mural Cemetery.

10 Follow the long gravel and grass path as it turns into a road. At the bottom of the valley the road swings left then right. Then, at the next junction, on the right note the domed 'Byzantine' style mausoleum of the Baldwin family ★. Turn left here, taking the grass path up the bank. Continue ahead until you reach the gate in the wall and the steps you came up earlier. At the bottom of the steps, turn right and return to Lewes Road.

ᴀᴢ walk eleven

Grandstand Views

The racecourse and a Neolithic camp.

This is a taste of the countryside that's easily accessible from the city centre. Rising quickly from the Kemptown seafront up to the South Downs, we are rewarded with dramatic and panoramic views over Brighton, the countryside and the English Channel. This also makes it one of the most exposed walks – choose a day when the wind is kind.

Whitehawk Camp, built around 3500 BC, is one of Britain's earliest Stone Age monuments. The purpose of the site is not fully understood, but evidence of human burials and feasting have been found. Despite the intrusion of the racecourse and a road, a section of banks and ditches can be seen on our walk.

Most of the route then follows Brighton Racecourse, where horses have competed since the Duke of Cumberland's first meeting in 1783. It is one of Britain's more unusual racecourses – a U-shaped track perched on a hilltop with a housing estate in the middle – and its gradients and turns make it a unique test for a thoroughbred.

The walk continues through the rare chalk grassland of Whitehawk Hill Local Nature Reserve. But it is the views that really make this walk special: first to the west over the city (you can even see the Isle of Wight on a clear day), then north and east across the undulating South Downs and south for a bird's-eye perspective on the English Channel.

start / finish	Junction of Paston Place and Marine Parade
nearest postcode	BN2 1DJ
distance	4½ miles / 7.2 km
time	2 hours 30 minutes
terrain	Surfaced roads and paths, stony paths, grassland, one long steep hill.

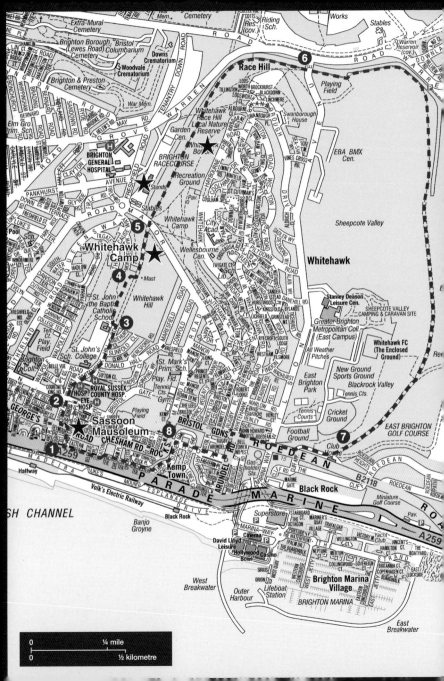

1 Start on Marine Parade and head up Paston Place. At the end on the right note the Indian-style Sassoon Mausoleum ★ now a cabaret club. Turn left onto St George's Road and take the next right up Abbey Road, passing in front of St George's Church.

2 Carefully cross the busy Eastern Road and continue uphill on Upper Abbey Road. Take the next right onto Whitehawk Hill Road and continue up the steep hill with the Royal Sussex Hospital on your right. After the school, continue straight ahead up Whitehawk Hill Road (don't follow the road to the right) and over the mini-roundabout.

3 Near the top of the hill, where the road turns into a gravel track, turn left onto a footpath and almost immediately take the path that goes right. Enjoy views to your left of Brighton and beyond, then take the fork to the right heading towards the communications tower.

4 When the path emerges onto a wide gravel track, turn left and pass the tower. The racecourse and the grandstand ★ now come into view with the pulling-up area to your left. You are now walking through the centre of the Neolithic Whitehawk Camp ★ – look to the grassy area on your right to see the remains of the 5,500-year-old ditches and banks.

5 Cross the road and you will see the information board about Whitehawk Camp on your right. Continue ahead, taking the lower path to the right of the line of trees. This area is the Whitehawk Hill Local Nature Reserve ★ . After about 500 yards (450 metres) you cross a concrete path, and soon after this, take the left fork to bring you up closer to the white rails of the racecourse. Follow the path next to the racecourse for another 500 yards (450 metres).

6 Cross Wilson Avenue and go through the gate, then follow the path for another mile and a half (2.4 km) as it gradually turns right towards the sea and continues beyond the end of the racecourse. Enjoy the views over the downs to your left.

7 At the end of the path, go through the gate and walk through the golf club car park, following the drive round to the right which joins Roedean Road at the bottom. Continue along the right-hand pavement, over the crossroads, and at the mini-roundabout turn left onto Arundel Road. Take the first right onto Eastern Road.

8 Take the third turning on the left to walk down the western side of Sussex Square and Lewes Crescent. Just before the seafront road, turn right onto Chichester Terrace and follow the pavement in front of the seafront terraces for about 550 yards (500 metres) to return to your starting point.

ᴀz walk twelve

Hove Actually

Grand houses and bewitching backstreets.

Hove is the elegant residential west end of the city. The sprawling geography and lack of a clear centre can make it tricky for the casual visitor to get a handle on Hove, but this walk will lead you to some of the most agreeable spots in the entire city.

Just a hundred people lived here in 1801, then the 19th-century building boom saw Brighton spill westwards creating most of the Hove we see today. It remained, however, an independent town with its own borough council until a merger in 1997 created Brighton and Hove.

The spirit of independence remains, though. Keen to differentiate itself from its brash and saucy neighbour, you are likely to hear a resident say, 'Well, I'm from Hove actually…'. And, it is true, it is different here – it's a town of planned developments, wide straight avenues and fine domestic architecture.

Yet it is far from monotonous – the architectural detail is exuberant and inventive, quaint mews streets have been given quirky makeovers, the churches more than match the ambition of the houses, and the colourful beach huts are a photo-blogger's dream. And history abounds – Hove has a superb local museum, many of the so-called 'Brighton School' of pioneering filmmakers were based in Hove (actually) and you will see the grave of Sir George Everest, of mountain fame.

start / finish	Hove Promenade (seafront café opposite St John's Road)
nearest postcode	BN3 2FR
distance	3½ miles / 5.7 km
time	1 hour 30 minutes
terrain	Mostly paved roads and paths, some cobbled streets, no hills or steps.

HOVE

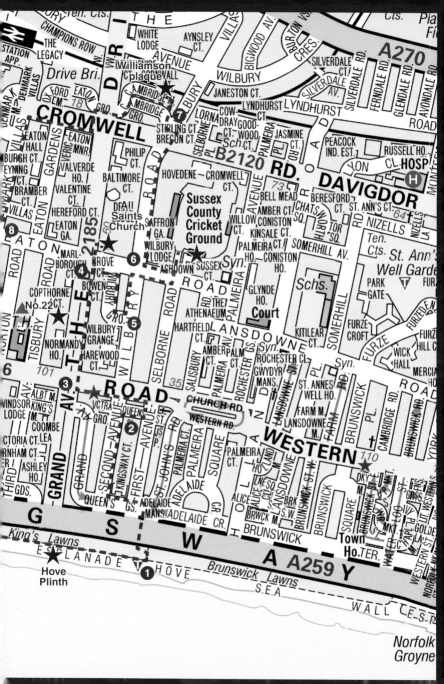

1 Starting on Hove promenade, walk to the right of the café at the end of the row of beach huts, towards the main road and the pedestrian crossing. Cross the road to the far pavement and turn left. Take the second right up Second Avenue. This street has some fine examples of late 19th-century town houses built in pale yellow brick from the local gault clay, and, like much of Hove, the houses display some elaborate and interesting architectural details.

2 Just before you reach the top of the street, turn right into cobbled Queens Place, built as stables for the neighbouring houses, now converted to residential properties, small offices and motor repair garages. At the end, turn left, noting the flint church and garden on your right, St John's. Turn left again onto Church Road, the main spine through Hove where some of the city's best restaurants can be found – you might want to explore more of this road later on.

3 Turn right at the second junction, crossing Church Road at the traffic lights and heading up The Drive on the right-hand side. The Drive has a mixture of 19th-century grand town houses and 20th-century flats. Note number 22 ★ on the left-hand side, a red brick and terracotta apartment block with a castellated tower, domes and elaborate chimneys.

4 At the next junction look across to the cathedral-like All Saints Church ★, the parish church for Hove. If you wish, cross over to view the west entrance and (if open) the impressive stone interior, then retrace your steps to walk east along Eaton Road on the right-hand side. When you are just past the east end of the church, turn right onto the narrow cobbled Wilbury Grove – stables and a riding school until the 1960s, now a charming mix of garages, offices and homes.

5 When you come out onto Wilbury Road, turn left, then right at the next junction along Eaton Road until you reach the entrance of Sussex County Cricket Club ★, home to the oldest of the first class county clubs. On non-match days you can visit the Sussex Cricket Club shop. Turn round and head back along Eaton Road on the right-hand side.

6 Take the next right onto Wilbury Road. Here, some of the grandest Hove villas can be found. At the top of the road cross Cromwell Road, then turn left and cross again. On the other side bear right to take a small road that leads behind the houses – Cambridge Grove. At the end, follow the street round to the left, then look right to see a house set back from the others with a plaque commemorating cinematographer James Williamson ★, who, at the beginning of the 20th century, is credited with some of the first close-up shots in film history.

7 Retrace your steps and turn right down the long, straight row of garages – again, former stables. At the end, turn left up to the traffic lights. Cross twice at the lights to reach the opposite corner and walk west along the left-hand side of Cromwell Road. When you reach the mini-roundabout at the end, turn left down Denmark Villas, an attractive street of Italianate-style villas and some fine front gardens.

8 After you cross the junction with Eaton Villas, cross to the right side of Denmark Villas and continue to the next junction, where you turn right onto Blatchington Road. Cross to the left-hand side at the pedestrian lights, where you pass the end of George Street, Hove's main shopping street.

9 Take the second left onto Belfast Street. Follow this street as it bends right and becomes Stirling Place. At the next junction, near the pub, turn left into a footpath that takes you under an arch. When you emerge onto Connaught Road, continue straight ahead to the junction with the busy Sackville Road. Cross over and walk ahead down Pembroke Crescent.

10 Take the second left down Pembroke Gardens. After the last house, the gardens of Hove Museum ★ open out to your left. Take the path through the gate and walk round to the entrance of the museum, which has displays on the local pioneers of film, toys, crafts and local history, and entry

is free. Exiting the museum, note Jaipur Gate in the museum grounds – paid for by the Maharaja of Jaipur, it originally formed the entrance to a London exhibition in 1886.

11 Turn left onto New Church Road. Continue for about 550 yards (500 metres) until you reach St Andrew's Church, Hove's first parish church before the original hamlet was engulfed by the 19th-century expansion of Brighton. Enter the churchyard through the furthest gap in the wall, by the bus stop. Here is the grave of Sir George Everest ★ , after whom Mount Everest is named: walk into the churchyard and look left, three rows back from the path there are three identical round-topped headstones – Everest's is the middle one.

12 Exiting the churchyard, continue along Church Road, crossing to the south side at the pedestrian lights. Turn right at the second turning and head down Medina Villas, another fine display of Hove domestic architecture. At the end, turn left and cross Kingsway at the pedestrian lights and head to the seafront promenade and turn left. Along the promenade enjoy the colourful Hove beach huts and Hove Plinth sculpture ★ , representing some of the icons of Hove that we have seen on our walk today, before returning to the café.

A̅Z walk thirteen

Smugglers, Artists and Cliffs

A spectacular coastal path to Rottingdean village.

This grand circuit leaves the city via Brighton Marina along the stunning undercliff walkway to the picture-perfect village of Rottingdean, then back over the downs through the hidden village of Ovingdean.

We start at Brighton Marina with its mixture of boating, retail and leisure. We then head east under the dazzling white chalk cliffs (bring your sunglasses!) to the coastal village of Rottingdean. Some of its buildings date to the 16th century when the village prospered on sheep farming and smuggling. In the 19th century Rottingdean attracted artists and writers, including Rudyard Kipling – author of *The Jungle Book* – whose garden is free and open to visitors.

Rottingdean Museum (open Wednesday to Sunday) occupies the former house of artist William Nicholson. You can learn about the bizarre 'Daddy Long Legs' aquatic railway-on-stilts that once connected the village to Brighton. You can see Rudyard Kipling's reconstructed study and a room dedicated to Kipling's uncle, Edward Burne-Jones, the Pre-Raphaelite painter whose stained glass windows can be seen here in the 13th-century village church.

We then climb to the iconic Rottingdean Windmill, built to grind the village corn in 1802, which stands proud on a hilltop overlooking the sea. Afterwards we venture into what Kipling called the 'blunt, bow-headed, whale-backed downs', passing through timeless Ovingdean with its exquisite 12th-century church, then returning to the city with high views over the English Channel.

start / finish	Brighton Marina, by the supermarket
nearest postcode	BN2 5UU
distance	6¼ miles / 10 km
time	3 hours 30 minutes
terrain	Surfaced paths, grassy and stony rural footpaths, steep hills, stiles, steps.

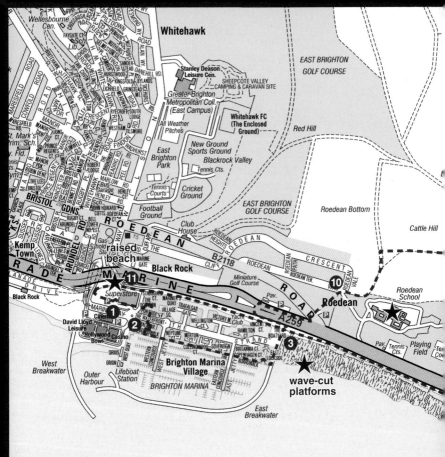

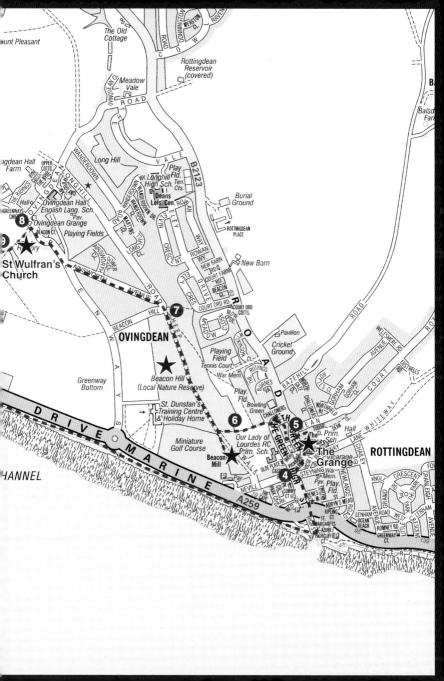

1 Start by the supermarket entrance, with the cliff in the distance to your left, and walk along the right-hand side of the supermarket. Cross the small side road then bear slightly left to enter the pedestrianized shopping area 'The Village'. When you emerge at an open area with some water in front of you, turn right, then cross at the zebra crossing. Turn left then immediately right to go up some steps signposted to 'The Boardwalk'.

2 At the top of the steps, go between the buildings to emerge onto the boardwalk and turn left. Continue past the restaurants and cafés to the far side of the marina. When the path ends at a car park, follow the yellow lines across the lock. On the other side, bear right to the corner of the car park to find a small set of steps up to the marina wall. Turn left towards the cliffs.

3 When you reach the undercliff path, turn right. If the tide is low, note the wave-cut chalk platforms ★ (the base of eroded cliffs) between the beach and the sea, a rare coastal habitat. Continue for about 1¾ miles (2.7 km) until you reach the buildings of Rottingdean. Walk up the sloped access road to the traffic lights. Use the right-hand crossing and continue ahead into High Street, with its traditional flint cottages.

4 Turn right up Vicarage Lane. Soon on your right is The Grange, once home to artist William Nicholson, now a library, an excellent free museum and a café. Continue past the village green and pond to St Margaret's Church – usually open to visitors, with seven stained glass windows by Burne-Jones, whose ashes are buried in the churchyard and marked with a plaque to the right of the door. Other burials here include Thin Lizzy guitarist Gary Moore, by the far east wall of the churchyard.

5 Exiting the churchyard, cross the road onto the village green. Note the large house on your right, The Elms, once home to Rudyard Kipling. Continue to the far side of the green to view the row of houses straight ahead: Prospect House, Aubrey Cottage and North End House. Formerly one large property, this was the home of Burne-Jones, and later Enid Bagnold, author of *National Velvet*, and her husband Roderick Jones, chairman of news agency Reuters. Staying on the grass, turn right and go through the arch into Kipling's Gardens. Explore the garden, and then follow the main path past the croquet lawn and through the arch to the road. Cross the road and turn left. At the bend, bear right onto a stony lane and follow this path up the hill.

6 You emerge onto a grassy hill. Continue ahead as the windmill appears on your left. At the top of the hill continue over the first path and turn left onto the second path which takes you to the front of the windmill ★. Retrace your steps then follow this main grassy path across Beacon Hill Nature Reserve ★ for about half a mile (800 metres) until you reach the road.

7 Go through the gate and continue ahead along Longhill Road, then almost immediately bear left down Ainsworth Avenue. At the end, turn right and cross so you are walking on the left-hand side of the road. Continue through Ovingdean village until the turning towards the church on the left. Opposite this turning is Ovingdean Grange, a 16th-century manor house which gave its name to a novel by William Harrison Ainsworth.

8 Turn left and walk up to St Wulfran's Church ★ – built around 1100 and possibly the oldest building within the boundaries of Brighton and Hove. The churchyard is the resting place of Helena Normanton, the UK's first woman barrister, and Magnus Volk, inventor of Brighton's Volk's and 'Daddy Long Legs' railways. Leave the churchyard the same way you came. Immediately after the church gate, turn left and take the steps over the wall, then turn left and follow the wall up to the top left corner of the field.

9 Go over the stile and continue ahead up the hill. Follow the footpath as it continues along the fence on your right. On your left in the distance you will see the buildings of Roedean ★, a top private school. Continue down the hill to the end of the path, turn left and follow the broad path as it bends right towards a road.

10 When you reach the road, take the path that goes diagonally across the grass to the junction of Roedean Road and Marine Drive. Turn right along the pavement of Marine Drive, the main seafront road. At the traffic lights, cross over towards the cliffs then continue ahead down the wide path that cuts down the cliff and joins the undercliff path. Turn right along the path past the marina.

11 Near the end of the path, note the sandy-coloured section of cliff and the information board that indicates a 250,000-year-old raised beach ★ and ice-age sediments. Continue until you reach a set of steps that take you down to the supermarket car park and back to the starting point.

⚍ walk fourteen

Downs and Gowns

The villages of Stanmer and Falmer.

This is a varied walk between the outer edge of Brighton and the South Downs, with the contrasting delights of a historic park, countryside and monumental modern architecture.

Stanmer Park was created in the 18th century as a private estate around Stanmer House to include its own church, landscaped park, private farm and village. Now owned by the council, it is the city's largest park and a popular weekend destination with its well-preserved buildings, tea rooms and community horticultural projects.

We then take in the University of Sussex, the only UK university located entirely within a national park and one of the most successful examples of a 1960s campus with its innovative brickwork architecture by Sir Basil Spence (of Coventry Cathedral fame). Next we will visit Falmer, a peaceful downland village until the 1970s when the A27 dual carriageway split it in two. Despite all the modern intrusions, Falmer maintains a timeless rural charm.

The walk finishes at Falmer Stadium, currently known as the American Express Community Stadium, which was built as the home of Brighton and Hove Albion in 2011 and saw the club's rise to football's Premier League. The 32,000-seat venue is an impressive sight nestled in the rolling hills. Unless you are attending a match, it is advised to do this walk on a non-match day to avoid travel disruption.

start / finish	Falmer Railway Station, Station Approach
nearest postcode	BN1 9SD
distance	4¼ miles / 6.7 km
time	2 hours
terrain	Paved roads and paths, grass and dirt footpaths, some short steep hills and steps.

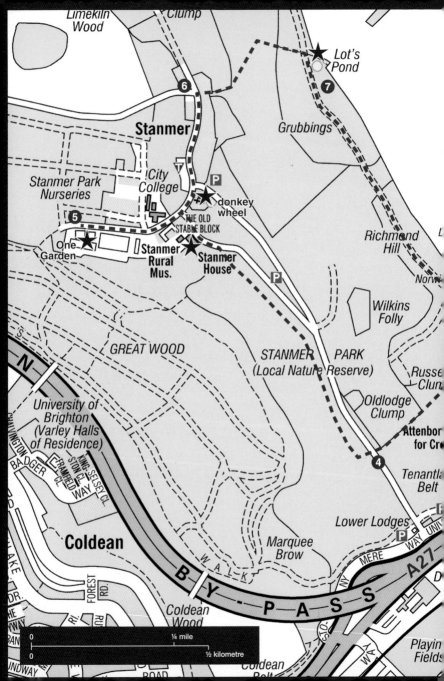

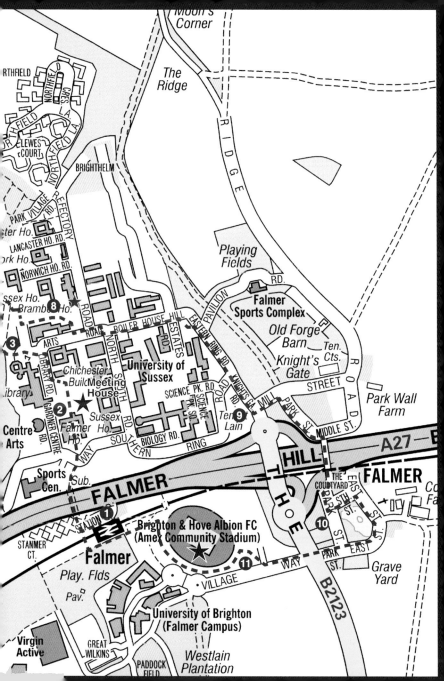

1 Starting with the ticket office exit of Falmer Station behind you, go ahead and down the steps through the pedestrian tunnel towards the University of Sussex. Cross the zebra crossing and continue ahead into the moated courtyard of Falmer House. You emerge on the other side into an open square. Note on your right the circular Meeting House ★ , inspired by local oast (hop-drying) houses.

2 Continue ahead and, just before the door of the Arts A building, take the small path that goes round to the left and up the steps. Join the pavement beside the small road as it continues uphill. Turn left at the road junction, then left again up a car park approach road. Where the road swings left, continue ahead onto a surfaced footpath towards the trees.

3 Where this surfaced path makes a sharp right-hand turn, continue ahead to take the path up the hill into the woods. You will soon join a wider path that emerges after about 110 yards (100 metres) into a meadow and Stanmer Park. Continue straight ahead down the hill diagonally across the meadow, joining a gravel path next to a fence on your right, which takes you to a road.

4 Follow the path across the road then turn right onto a wide gravel path. Follow this path for about half a mile (750 metres) until it joins the road which takes you in front of Stanmer House ★ , owned from 1722 to 1942 by the Pelham family, many of whom were politicians. At the road junction turn left and follow this road to the end, where you can visit One Garden ★ , a modern reinvention of an historic walled garden, run by a local agricultural college.

5 Retrace your steps then continue on this road to Stanmer Church. At the end of the churchyard turn right to see the small flint building housing a well and a rare donkey wheel ★ – like a giant hamster wheel which raised buckets of water using donkey power. With your back to the well house, take the road between the buildings and into Stanmer Village and continue to the end of the road.

6 After you pass the last cottage, turn right onto a footpath that takes you through a gate and up a hill. When the path opens out to a meadow, continue on the grassy path ahead as it bears slightly left towards the woodland at the top of the hill. Go through the gate and follow the main path into the woods, and, when this path crosses a wider path, turn right. Note on your left a dew pond ★ – a traditional artificial water store for livestock, common on Sussex chalk hilltops.

7 Follow this wide path to the end of the woodland and continue ahead through the gate across the meadow an into another wood. Continue for about ¼ mile (400 metres). At the waymarked junction keep left/straight ahead, and you soon see a car park ahead of you. You are now back at the university. Enter the car park, turn right and follow the exit road. Shortly after leaving the car park, take the wide flight of steps down to your left between the buildings.

8 At the bottom of the steps keep right and follow the narrow path beside the brick building as it swings right and joins Arts Road. Turn left to walk along Arts Road, cross to the right-hand pavement, and follow this road all the way up the hill. Keep to the right-hand side of the road as it eventually becomes Eastern Ring Road.

9 As you approach the large roundabout at the bottom of the hill, carefully cross the road to turn left into Mill Street, then take the first right into Park Street. You are now in the north part of Falmer village. At the bottom by the pub, take the pedestrian bridge across the dual carriageway. When you reach the other side bear right to join the southern section of Park Street. This soon opens out to the village green.

10 Turn left and follow the pond clockwise, passing St Laurence Church. At the road junction, continue ahead towards the traffic lights, walking along the right-hand pavement. Cross the main road using the two sets of pedestrian lights and continue ahead towards the football stadium ★ . Walk past the first car park entrance, then just before the bus stop, turn right into the car park. Then bear left towards a set of steps down to the wide walkway that rings the stadium.

11 Turn left and follow the stadium clockwise, taking the wide steps down to your right, where you can find the Brighton and Hove Albion shop. Opposite the shop, turn left to follow the wide concourse that goes downhill where you find Falmer Station ahead of you. Follow the signs and cross the footbridge to take you back to the starting point.

Aᴢ walk fifteen

Medieval Village in the Suburbs

Hidden treasures in Old Portslade.

Portslade was once one of the most important villages in the Brighton area. In 1801 it had a population of over 300, three times as many as Hove. Then, in the 20th century, the village was engulfed by the relentless growth of Brighton. Today, what most people think of as Portslade is a mile to the south – a busy suburb around the railway station and the shops of Boundary Road. But it is well worth making the trip up to the old village, which feels like a journey back in time.

You can visit a 12th-century church next to the ruins of one of the few remaining Norman manor houses in the country. The old High Street still evokes the days when Portslade was a sheep-farming community. In the 19th century, industry came in the form of the Portslade Brewery, whose repurposed buildings still dominate the village.

Ideally, you should do this walk on a day when Emmaus is open (Tuesday to Saturday at the time of writing), an interesting complex of second-hand shops, gardens and a café in the buildings of a former convent. Today it is a community of former homeless people who volunteer in the shops in exchange for support and housing.

There is a regular bus service between the city centre and the village.

start / finish	St Nicolas Church bus stop, junction of South Street and Manor Road
nearest postcode	BN41 2LE
distance	1¼ miles / 1.9 km
time	30 minutes
terrain	Paved roads and paths, one short grassy section (optional), one short hill.

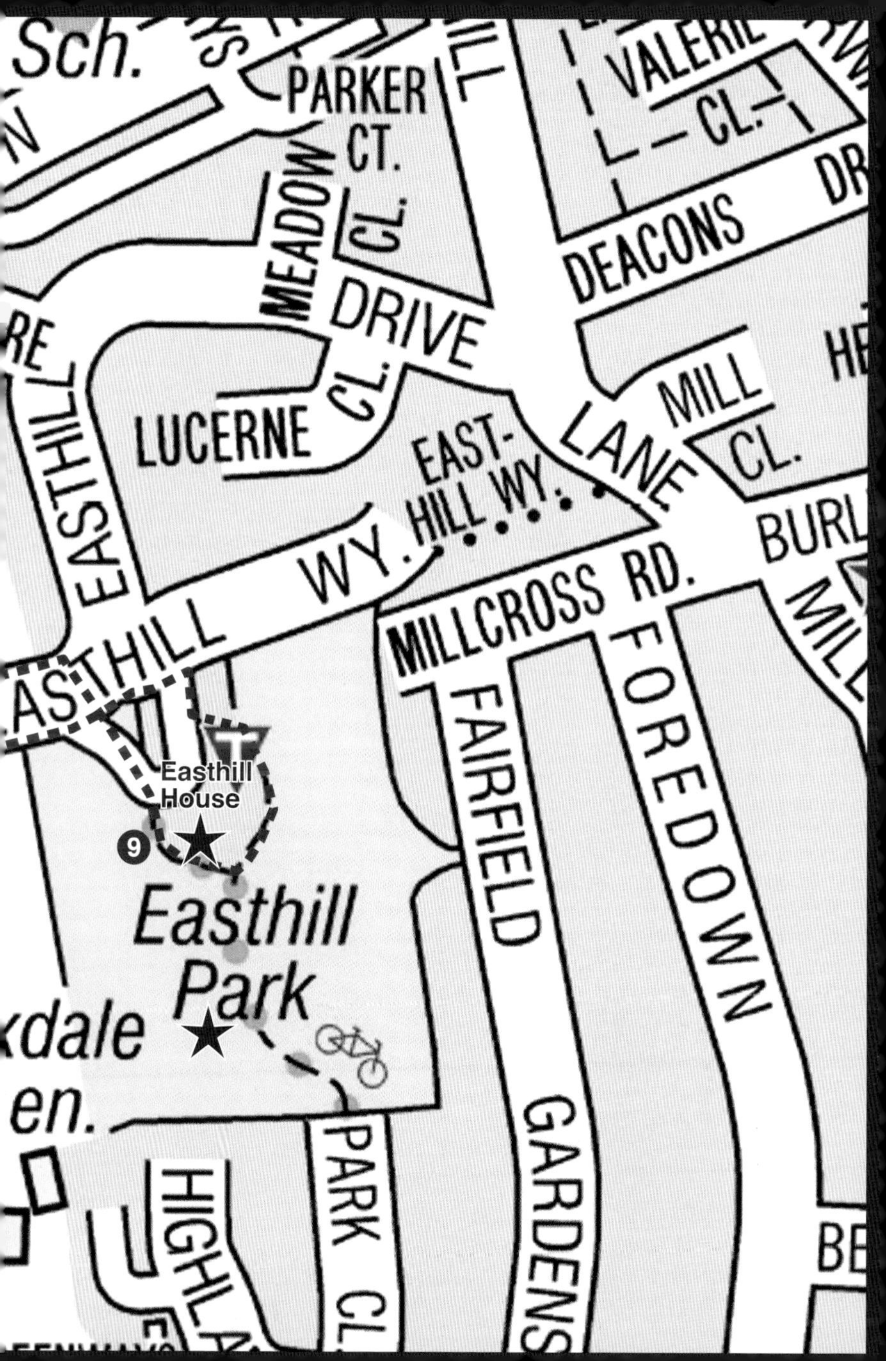

Sch.

PARKER
CT.

MEADOW CL.

PARKER CL.

DRIVE

VALERIE
CL.

DEACONS

DR

LUCERNE

EAST-
HILL WY.

WY. HILL WY.

LANE

MILL

CL.

HE

EASTHILL

EASTHILL

MILLCROSS RD.

FAIRFIELD

BURL

BE

MILL

Easthill
House

❾ ★

Easthill
Park

kdale
en.

★

FOREDOWN

HIGHLA

PARK CL.

GARDENS

BE

EENWAY

❶ Starting at the corner of South Street and Manor Road, turn up Manor Road and immediately take the path left towards St Nicolas Church ★. The church has parts dating back to the 12th century. Note the decorative carvings on many of the headstones in the churchyard, and the church roof made of Horsham stone, a type of sandstone local to West Sussex.

❷ When you are close to the church entrance porch, head right across the grass, round to the far corner (east end) of the church. Beyond the iron railings you can see a wall and window aperture of the now-ruined Portslade Old Manor ★ (1140s), one of the few remaining Norman manor houses in England. Retrace your steps to the path and out of the church gate to return to Manor Road.

❸ Turn right down South Street and continue as it bends right down the hill. Near the junction with High Street, note The Stags Head pub ★, dating from the late 17th century. Go straight ahead down the narrow South Street. The former Portslade Brewery building ★ (1880s) on your right dominates the village, with the older brewery buildings (mid-1800s) on your left.

❹ At the end of the road, ahead left, note the Old Malthouse ★ – barley grains were germinated here and the resulting malt was dropped from the timber projection into carts below to be brewed into beer. Retrace your steps past the brewery buildings again and turn left onto High Street. Here at the heart of the old village are some of the best-preserved historic cottages.

❺ At the top of the hill, note the large house on the left by the bend. Kemps ★, built by Edward Blaker in 1540, is the oldest inhabited house in the village, and remained in the Blaker family for 350 years. Turn round to take in the view down the High Street before continuing to the end of High Street past the old stables.

❻ Turn right onto Drove Road, ignore the first entrance on your right, and after a couple of cottages turn right into the main drive of Emmaus, if open. Walk ahead along the drive into the Emmaus ★ complex. On either side there are buildings housing the Secondhand Superstore and a café. Please keep to the public areas and respect the private residences of the community.

7 At the end of the drive, you can explore the garden areas on your right and straight ahead. On the right is the best view of the ruins of Portslade Old Manor ★ . Ahead, there is a sunken walled garden, with a locked, gated tunnel ★ leading under the road to a private garden. Retrace your steps to exit Emmaus the way you came.

8 Turn right onto Drove Road, then right again into Manor Road, taking care as there is no pavement. At the end of the Emmaus buildings on your right, note the former chapel, a reminder of Emmaus' historical use as a convent. At the end, turn left onto Easthill Way and then when you see the entrance to Easthill Park ★ on your right, cross over and walk up the driveway into the park.

9 Walk past Easthill House ★ , built by the Blaker family in 1848, now flats. The grounds of the house were opened as a public park in 1947. Feel free to explore the park, otherwise follow the path left after the house then left again. After the toilet block turn left then right to join the paved driveway leading out of the park. When you emerge onto Easthill Way, turn left and continue ahead, which leads you back to the starting point.

⒜⒵ walk sixteen

Chattri Memorial

A unique war memorial in a spectacular hillside setting.

This is a countryside ramble that takes us from the northern suburb of Patcham into the heart of the South Downs hills.

The focus of our walk is the Chattri, a war memorial set on a scenic hillside, accessible only on foot. In the First World War, soldiers from India served alongside British troops and many of the injured were treated in military hospitals in Brighton, including the Royal Pavilion. The 53 Hindu and Sikh soldiers who died during that time were carried up to this peaceful spot on the downs and cremated, and their ashes scattered in the English Channel. In 1921, a memorial was built on the cremation site in the form of a marble domed pavilion (*chattri* means 'umbrella' in Hindi, Punjabi and Urdu) and a service of remembrance is held here every June.

This walk also explores the countryside and the rounded hills of the South Downs, with distant views towards Brighton and the sea. It is very much a countryside hike with no shelter or facilities once you leave the starting point, so please dress for the weather and bring everything you need. Be aware that some paths might be rough or overgrown – walking shoes and long trousers are advised.

There is a regular bus service between the city centre and Mackie Avenue.

start / finish	Ladies Mile pub, Mackie Avenue, Patcham
nearest postcode	BN1 8RA
distance	5½ miles / 8.7 km
time	2 hours 30 minutes
terrain	Rural footpaths (possibly muddy), gravel tracks, paved roads, hills, stiles.

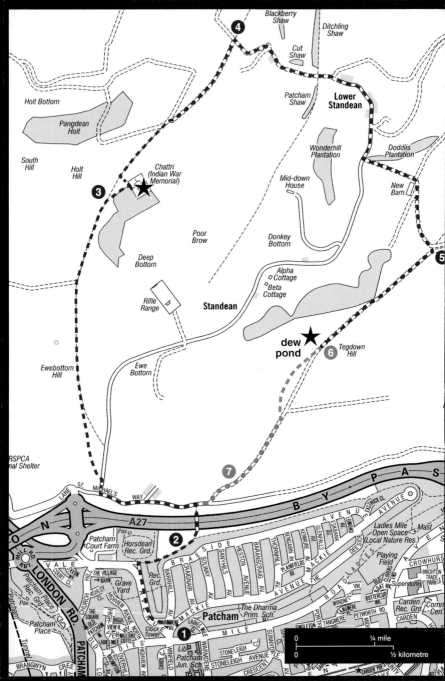

1 With the pub behind you, cross the road, passing to the right of the unusual 1930s Art Deco clock tower, and walk up Warmdene Avenue then right along Vale Avenue. Keep to the right-hand pavement and when the main road bends left, continue directly ahead towards the recreation ground. Just before the playing field, turn right onto the gravel path, keeping right as you continue straight ahead up the hill.

2 After about 330 yards (300 metres), near the top of the hill, there is a waymarked fork. Take the left path which soon takes you over a footbridge over the A27 road. At the end of the bridge turn left and walk along the road. After about a third of a mile (500 metres), at the top of the next hill, turn right at the road junction. Immediately ahead is a gate into a field signposted 'Public Bridleway to Chattri Memorial' – take this path diagonally across the field up the hill and continue for about a mile (1.6 km).

3 You will soon see the white dome of the Chattri ★ ahead to the right of the path. As you near the Chattri, take the wide grassy path that bears right and leads down to the entrance gate. Explore the memorial area, enjoy the views and perhaps rest on one of the benches, then exit through the same gate and turn right to rejoin the main path then turn right again.

4 After about half a mile (850 metres) at the four-way junction, turn right and follow this track as it winds down into the valley and the hamlet of Lower Standean, consisting of farm buildings and a couple of houses. After you pass the last building – the large house on the hill to your left – continue for another 220 yards (200 metres). Then, at the top of the next rise, turn left onto the farm track up the hill and past a barn.

5 About 330 yards (300 metres) after the barn, where the track bends left, take the waymarked footpath on the right through the gate, and walk along the left-hand side of the field, following the straight fence on your left. After a third of a mile (600 metres), where the fence bends left, continue in a straight line across the open access field, aiming just to the right of a small solitary tree.

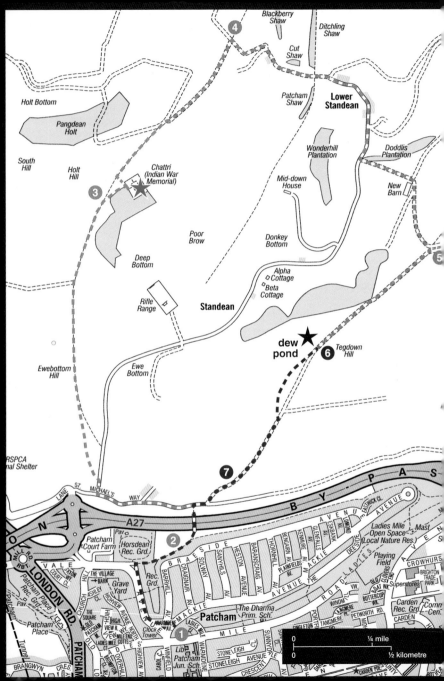

6 Immediately after the tree you pass a dew pond ★ on your right – an artificial pond which is a traditional source of water in these otherwise dry chalk hills. Continue ahead towards the fence on the far side of the field. Go through the wooden pedestrian gate and follow the track down the hill with the fence on your right.

7 Further down the hill, go through the gate to continue down the wide farm track. At the end of the track turn right onto the road. After a few steps turn left onto the pedestrian bridge you came over earlier. Then retrace your route back to the start: at the end of the bridge, continue to the path junction. Turn right then follow the left-hand path down the hill, then at the bottom turn left onto Vale Avenue and left again onto Warmdene Avenue.

ꭺꮓ walk seventeen

'The Grandest View in the World'

Brighton's favourite beauty spot.

Devil's Dyke, on the high northern escarpment of the South Downs, was said by painter John Constable to be 'the grandest view in the world', commanding vistas as far as Oxfordshire. The Dyke itself is Sussex's Grand Canyon – a deep dry valley which, according to legend, was scooped out by Satan trying to drown the inland churches with seawater, thwarted only by an elderly lady brandishing a candle.

This walk also takes you beyond the view and shows you the Devil's Dyke that many visitors don't notice. The precious chalk grassland (half the world's chalk grassland is in southern England) is the product of 3,000 years of sheep farming and home to rare species of butterfly and orchid. Human history is here too. We can see parts of the huge Iron Age fort that once ringed this hilltop. In the valley, the land has been worked for centuries in the hidden hamlet of Saddlescombe Farm, now overseen by the National Trust. For Victorian holidaymakers, Devil's Dyke was an amusement park – we can see remnants of some of its engineering projects – while in the Second World War soldiers from Canada, Australia and New Zealand camped and trained here.

Today the main visitor facility is a large pub – a welcome start and end to our walk. Although this route is not very long, the hills make it quite strenuous, and the steep sections make sensible walking shoes advisable.

A limited bus service operates between Brighton and Devil's Dyke.

start / finish	Devil's Dyke bus stop (opposite Devil's Dyke pub)
nearest postcode	BN1 8YJ
distance	3½ miles / 5.5 km
time	2 hours
terrain	Grass and stony footpaths, long steep hills, stiles. Some paths may be muddy and slippery.

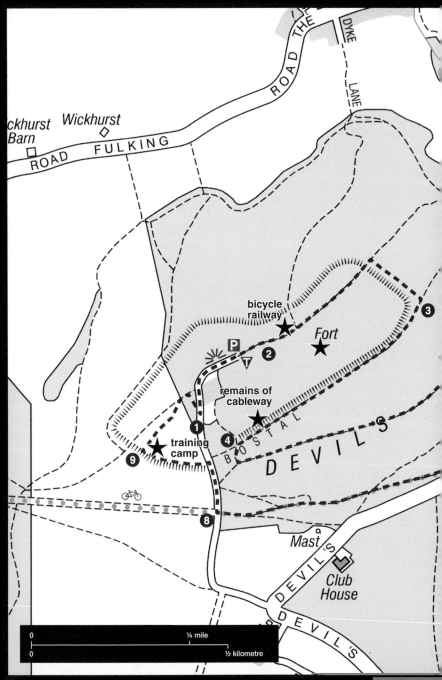

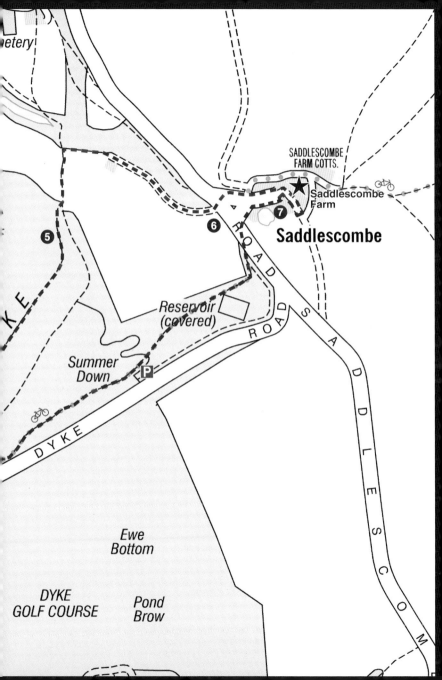

1 Starting from Devil's Dyke bus stop, continue along the left-hand side of the road towards the car park with the pub on your right. Soon you will see extensive views to the north and a viewpoint with information boards. Continue to the end of the car park towards the far right corner and take the signposted grassy footpath straight ahead along the top of the hill.

2 Continue ahead and bear slightly left at a fork. After about 110 yards (100 metres) you walk through a circular earthwork. This is the remains of one of the 19th-century amusements, where people rode bicycles around a miniature circular railway ★ (it didn't catch on). Continue ahead for about 220 yards (200 metres) to the end of the path then turn right. Note on your right the earthworks from the Iron Age hill fort ★ , which enclosed most of this hilltop.

3 Down the hill, you meet a wider stony track. Turn right and follow this track along the side of the hill for about a third of a mile (500 metres), and enjoy views to the left over the Devil's Dyke valley. Towards the end of the valley, the path passes the concrete foundation of another Victorian ride, Britain's first aerial cable car ★ (1894), which took passengers across the valley, where another concrete platform can be seen.

4 When you approach the trees at the end of the valley, turn left down a wide stony path and through the gate. At the lowest point turn left and walk down along the bottom of the valley. Take it slowly – it is deceptively steep here. Follow the bottom of the valley all the way down and round as it curves left.

5 After the left bend in the valley, head for the gate forward right, leading into a tree-lined bridleway. After about 110 yards (100 metres), at the waymarked junction, take the path uphill to the right and continue ahead over the stile. This eventually becomes a surfaced farm road – follow this until it ends at a busy public road.

6 Go through either the gate or the stile and then, watching out for fast cars, cross the road and walk up the entrance road to Saddlescombe Farm ★. At the fork in the track there is an information barn, seasonal café and toilets. Feel free to walk further and look at the farm buildings and hamlet from the track, but please be aware that this is a working farm – you would need to keep to the public areas and respect the privacy of the residents.

7 Go back the way you came, and when you reach the main road, cross over and turn left through the small car park and continue on the main track up the hill. You are now on the South Downs Way, the popular hiking trail which stretches from Eastbourne to Winchester.

8 After about a mile (1.6 km), you reach a road – turn right and walk along the right-hand side. After a short distance, turn left over the stile onto the waymarked footpath. This takes you alongside the ditch and rampart of the Iron Age hill fort towards a ruined brick building, a relic from the Second World War, when Devil's Dyke was used by soldiers to set up defensive positions and train for D-Day ★.

9 Turn right behind the building so that you are now walking towards the pub with spectacular views again to your left. When you reach the pub, you will find your starting point a short distance to your right.

ᴀᴢ walk eighteen
A Tale of Two Telscombes

A clifftop suburb and a remote downland village.

We first explore the chalk cliff coast and the 20th-century suburban merged towns of Telscombe Cliffs and Peacehaven. Created by speculator Charles Neville after he offered 'free' plots of land in a newspaper competition, the lucky recipients were then stung for an inflated conveyancing fee. The resulting scandal ironically brought more publicity, and thousands of 'pioneers' came to build their own homes in unregulated 'plotlands'. Further scandal ensued when it became clear how much pristine downland had been lost forever, and the outcry led to new national planning laws. Today the original buildings have been replaced, but the merged towns still retain a hint of a frontier settlement.

We then head to the hidden countryside hamlet of Telscombe Village. Although only a mile from Telscombe Cliffs, there's no direct road link – it's a nine-mile car journey via Newhaven. And it feels a world away: with a population of 50 people clustered around an 11th-century church, it is seemingly lost in time. This is thanks to racehorse trainer Ambrose Gorham who, after winning the Grand National in 1902, bought much of the village and bequeathed it to Brighton Council in 1936 on condition its rural character was preserved. The last stretch of our walk is on Telscombe Tye – the only undeveloped coastal downland between Brighton and Newhaven, and the perfect place to ponder the contrasting fate of the two Telscombes.

There is a regular bus service between the city centre and Telscombe Cliffs.

start / finish	Smuggler's Rest pub, South Coast Road, Telscombe Cliffs
nearest postcode	BN10 7BE
distance	5¼ miles / 8.6 km
time	2 hours 30 minutes
terrain	Surfaced roads and paths, grass and dirt paths (possibly muddy), some moderate hills.

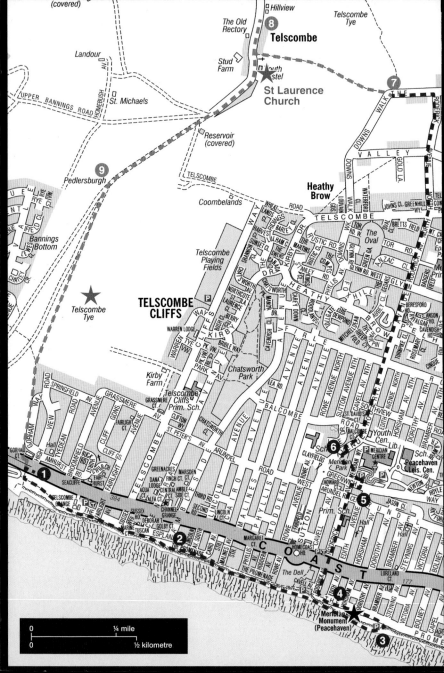

❶ Starting on the road looking towards the Smuggler's Rest pub, take the footpath a short distance to the right of the pub, then turn left on the path signposted 'England Coast Path' to head east along the clifftops. The undulating ground levels out to a wide grass promenade between the houses of Telscombe Cliffs and the sea.

❷ After about a third of a mile (500 metres), the path narrows to a gravel track then opens out to a park. Take the road that cuts down to your right through the cliffs, turn left at the bottom, and continue your journey eastwards along the undercliff walk, built as both a recreational walkway and to protect the town from erosion.

❸ After about half a mile (800 metres) take the ramp back up to the clifftop and turn left along the path with the houses of Peacehaven on your right. Head towards the Meridian Monument ★, marking the Greenwich Meridian, zero degrees longitude. Note the plaques, including one mentioning the founder of Peacehaven, Charles Neville, and distances to the colonial capital cities.

❹ Returning to the western hemisphere, continue along the clifftop, and take the second road on the right, Roderick Avenue. Cross the main road at the pedestrian lights and continue on the right-hand pavement for about 440 yards (400 metres). Here, you can get a sense of the grid layout that characterizes Peacehaven, and note the bungalows, each with its own individual style.

❺ Cross Greenwich Way at the pedestrian lights and continue north up Meridian Way. Very soon, look for an opening to a small park on your left, and the white Peacehaven and Telscombe War Memorial. Take the path to the right of the memorial which takes you out onto Sutton Avenue.

❻ Cross the road and turn right, and continue along the northern stretch of Roderick Avenue to the end. After about a mile (1.6 km), you leave the built-up area and Roderick Avenue continues as a country lane. Continue until the lane ends at a T-junction with The Lookout, and turn left.

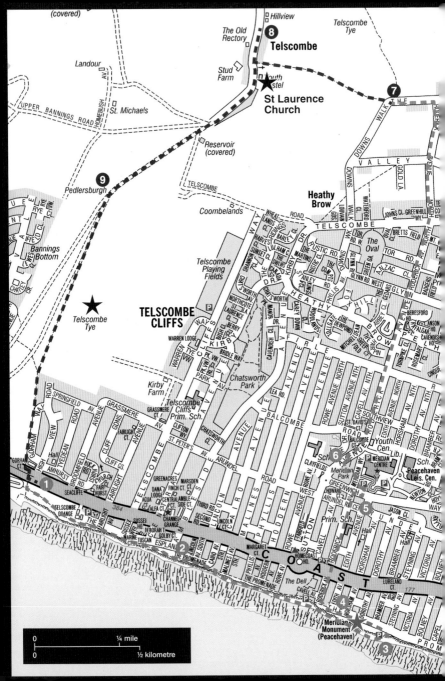

7 When the main track bends left, take the bridleway down to the right, and enjoy the views over the South Downs. The end of the path brings you into Telscombe Village. Turn right onto the road, taking care as there are no pavements. Soon, at the bottom of the hill on the right is Telscombe Village Club with a plaque informing us that it was the gift of Ambrose Gorham in 1924. The beech tree in front of the club was planted by the senior British officer in the First World War, Field Marshal Douglas Haig.

8 Turn round and head back past St Laurence Church ★ and the horse racing stables, and walk up the hill. At the top, cross the cattle grid and continue straight ahead, ignoring the forks on either side. After a short distance where the gravel road veers left, continue ahead on the straight grass and gravel track. You are now on Telscombe Tye ★ , an ancient common pasture, and the track you are on is the Old Funeral Road, traditionally used by coastal communities to reach St Laurence Church.

9 Continue straight ahead for about 545 yards (500 metres), keeping to the high ridge of the hill. As you descend towards the sea, you may see a faint grass path that bears slightly left. Don't worry if you miss the exact path on this open access grassland – just make your way towards the fence on your left-hand side some time over the next half mile (800 metres) or so. Follow the rough grass path beside the fence as it bears slightly left and takes you down past the edge of the houses until you reach the main coast road, then cross at the pedestrian lights to return to the pub.

△Z walk nineteen

Houseboat Magic

Shoreham by the sea.

Shoreham is an attractive town on the western edge of the Brighton and Hove conurbation, in an enviable location beside the downs, a river and a beach. It has long been one of the most important ports on the south coast, and today Shoreham Port to the east is still a busy working harbour.

The walk falls into three parts. First the town, with an impressive church and historic flint buildings, including one of the country's oldest buildings, the 12th-century home of the Marlipins Museum. We cross the estuary of the River Adur to visit an unusual community of about fifty houseboats. With its origins in the 1920s, it gained in popularity after the 1960s as many people sought alternative ways of living. Every boat is different, and, free of the planning rules that apply on dry land, many of them incorporate recycled materials. The anarchy, exuberance and creativity feels a world away from the neat town on the opposite bank.

The third part of the walk is along Shoreham Beach. The wide shingle vegetated bank is a local nature reserve, and we can enjoy views along the coast and a variety of modern designer homes.

Due to some narrow, unfenced riverside paths and the exposed coastal location, it is recommended that you do this walk in daylight and good weather.

start / finish	Shoreham-by-Sea Railway Station, Station Approach, Shoreham-by-Sea
nearest postcode	BN43 5WX
distance	2½ miles / 4 km
time	1 hour 15 minutes
terrain	Surfaced roads and paths, shingle beach (optional), two short sets of steps (optional), no hills.

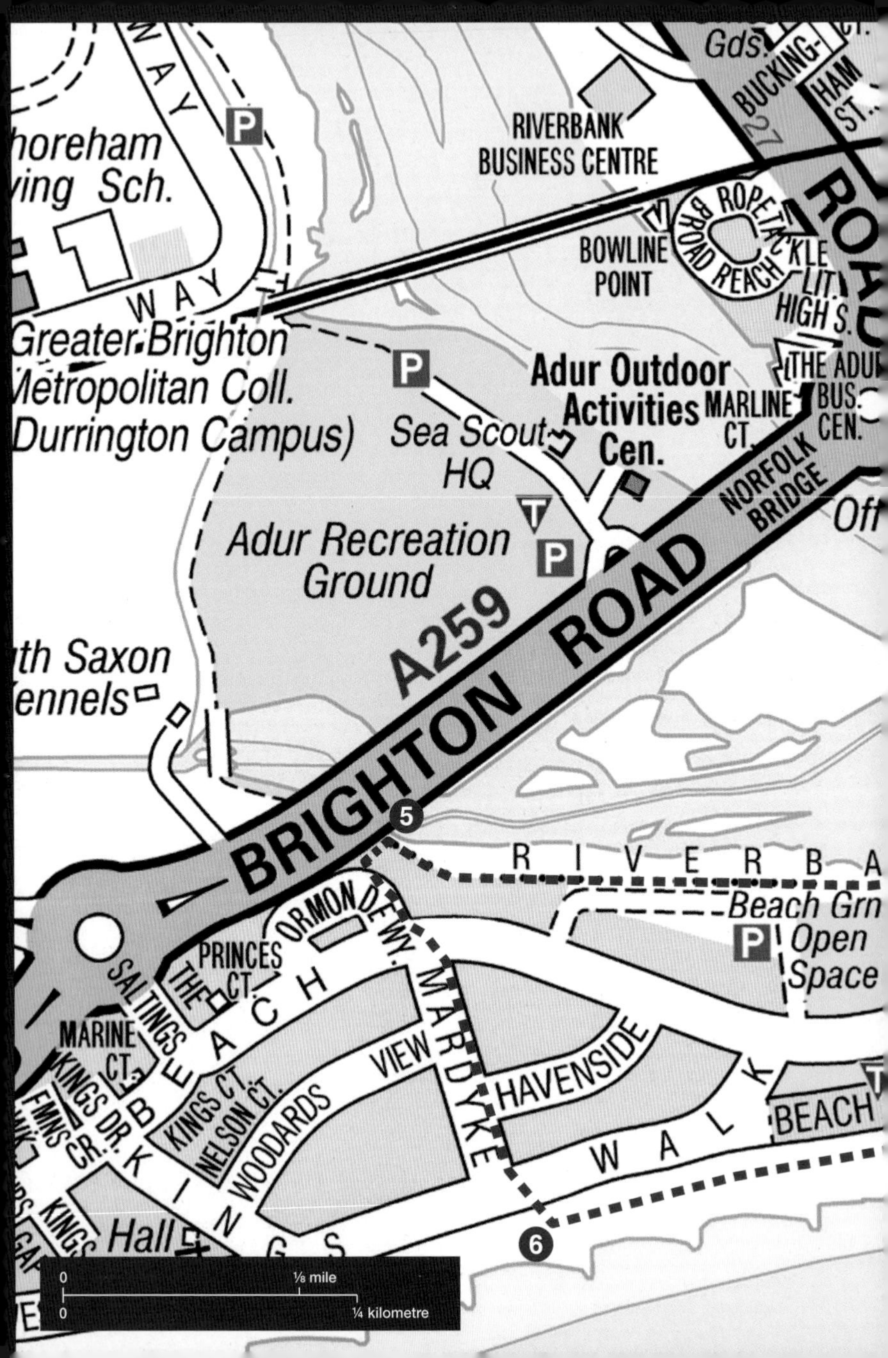

Gds.

BUCKING-

HAM ST.

CT.

27

ROAD

RIVERBANK
BUSINESS CENTRE

P

horeham
ving Sch.

WAY

BOWLINE
POINT

BB ROPETACKLE
ROAD REACH

KLE
LIT.
HIGH S.

THE ADUR
BUS.
CEN.

Greater Brighton
Metropolitan Coll.
(Durrington Campus)

WAY

P

Sea Scout
HQ

Adur Outdoor
Activities
Cen.

MARLINE
CT.

NORFOLK
BRIDGE

Off

T

P

Adur Recreation
Ground

T

th Saxon
Kennels

A259

BRIGHTON ROAD

5

RIVERBA

Beach Grn
Open
Space

P

ORMONDE WY.

PRINCES
CT.

THE BEACH

MARINE
CT.

KINGS DR.

FMNS.

KINGS CR.

KINGS CT.

NELSON CT.

WOODARDS

VIEW

MARDYKE

HAVENSIDE

WALK

BEACH

T

KINGS GAP

Hall

6

0   ⅛ mile

0   ¼ kilometre

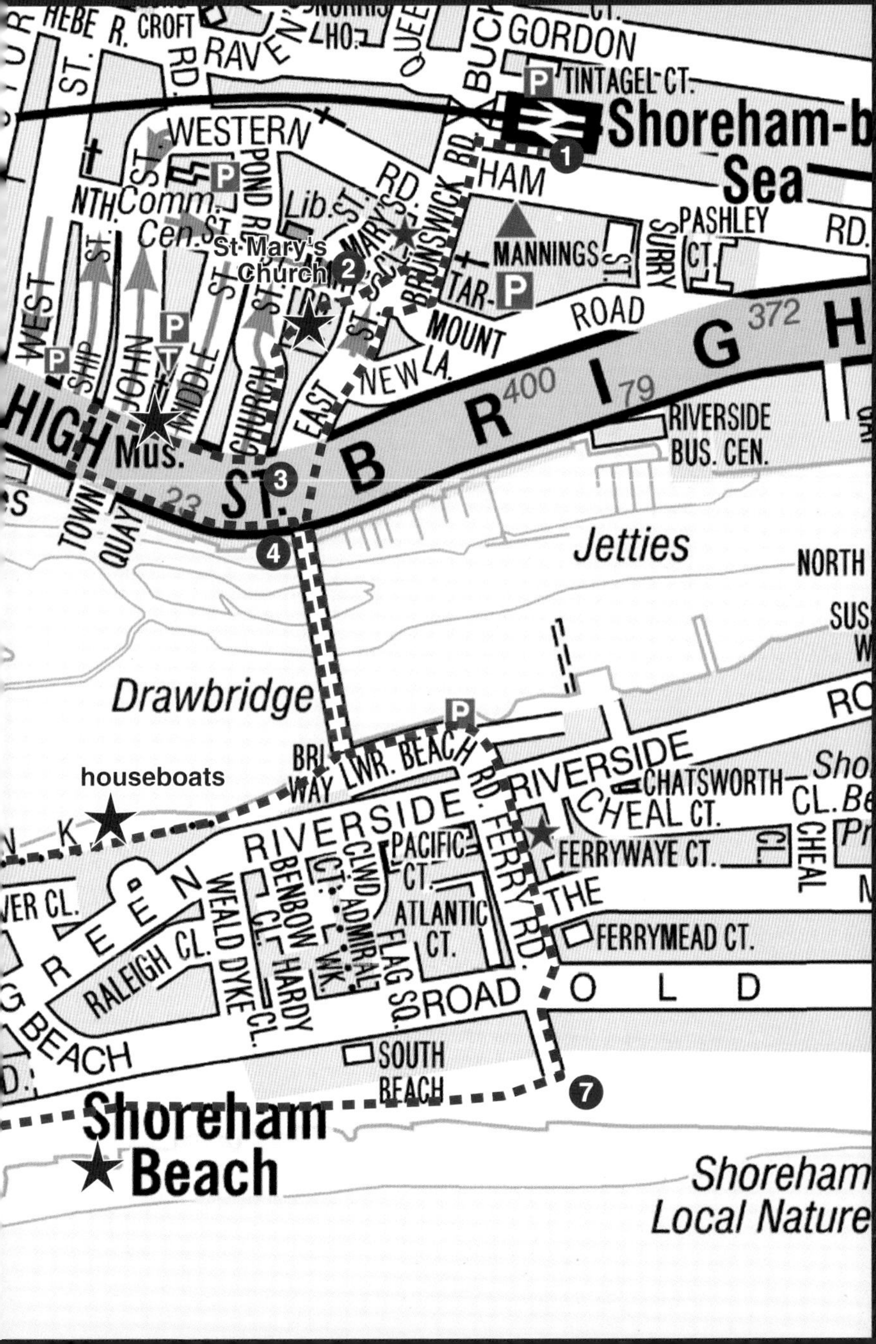

GORDON

HEBE R. CROFT

RAVEN

TINTAGEL CT.

Shoreham-by-Sea

WESTERN

Comm.
Cen.

MANNINGS

PASHLEY
SURRY

RD.

St Mary's
Church

Lib.

MOUNT

NEW LA.

ROAD

BRIGHT

RIVERSIDE
BUS. CEN.

HIGH

Mus.

ST.

Jetties

NORTH

Drawbridge

houseboats

BRI.
WAY

LWR. BEACH

RIVERSIDE

PACIFIC
CT.

CHATSWORTH
CHEAL CT.

FERRYWAYE CT.

CHEAL

RIVERSIDE

BENBOW

CLWD.
CT.

ADMIRAL
WK.

ATLANTIC
CT.

THE

FERRYMEAD CT.

RALEIGH CL.

WEALD DYKE CL.

FLAG SQ.

FERRY RD.

ROAD

OLD

SOUTH
BEACH

Shoreham
Beach

Shoreham
Local Nature

① Starting by the main (south) entrance of Shoreham Station, leave the station approach road and turn left onto Brunswick Road. At the end of the straight section, turn right onto St Mary's Road and you will see St Mary's Church ★ ahead. In contrast to the surrounding cottages, the church seems large, but it was originally more than twice this size – the nave was demolished in the 17th century, leaving a T-shaped rump.

② Enter the churchyard and follow the path towards the opposite corner. As you pass the west door of the church, note a ruined section of the former nave over to your right. Exit the churchyard and walk down Church Street, which has some splendid 18th-century flint cobble houses. There is a plaque on number 18 to Captain Henry Roberts, cartographer on James Cook's expeditions to the Pacific Ocean.

③ At the end, turn right on to High Street. On the next corner is the chequerboard stone and flint Marlipins Museum ★ – built possibly as a customs house in the 12th and 13th centuries, it is one of the oldest non-religious buildings in the country still in use. Today it contains a local history museum. Continue to the pedestrian lights, cross and turn left, so you are heading back east.

④ After about 220 yards (200 metres), cross the footbridge over the River Adur with views left towards Shoreham

Port and right across the tidal estuary. At the end of the bridge turn right and follow the riverside path. Watch out for unfenced drops on this narrow section of path as you pass nearly fifty houseboats ★, the largest of which is a German minesweeper from the Second World War. Please stay on the path and respect the privacy of the residents.

⑤ When the path ends at a road, turn left then left again down to Ormonde Way. At the end bear left as you cross the road and head up Mardyke until you reach Shoreham Beach ★. You can walk up the shingle bank onto the beach to enjoy views right to Worthing Pier and left to Brighton.

⑥ Walk east, with the sea on your right. You can walk along the top of the bank – a rare habitat of vegetated shingle – or for easier terrain stick to the pavement (you will get the views later on). Whichever way you take, immediately after the beach huts, join the boardwalk path to continue your way along the beach, past some enviable modern houses.

⑦ At the crossroads in the boardwalk, turn left. Continue past the shops on Ferry Road. At the end, cross the footbridge to return to the town centre. At the end of the bridge, continue over the pedestrian crossing onto East Street. As you pass the church again, return to the station the same way you came, by turning right onto St Mary's Road then left onto Brunswick Road.

A̅Z walk twenty

The Historic County Town

A perfect day trip to Lewes.

Only 8 miles (13 km) from Brighton and well served by public transport, Lewes makes for an easy and enjoyable day trip. Beautifully situated where the river Ouse cuts through the South Downs, Lewes is a traditional market town with a modern creative buzz. Despite its small size (population under 20,000), its status as the county town of East Sussex means that it punches well above its weight in terms of historical impact. The remains of Lewes Priory are impressive today, but they form just a tiny part of one of the most important religious houses in medieval England.

Back when Brighton was just a sleepy fishing town, Lewes was busy creating the modern world. The 1264 Battle of Lewes saw Simon de Montfort defeating King Henry III, which led to the first English parliament. Five hundred years later, Lewes customs officer Thomas Paine wrote the hugely influential *Common Sense* which powerfully articulated the cause of independence to the American people and is still the best-selling title in US history.

Although you could complete this circuit in an hour, you could easily extend this to half a day or more, particularly if you explore the visitor attractions en route – Lewes Castle, with its 360-degree views from the Keep, and Anne of Cleves House, a fascinating 15th-century house and museum – or stop at a pub for a pint of Harvey's.

start / finish	Lewes Railway Station, Station Road, Lewes
nearest postcode	BN7 2UP
distance	2½ miles / 4 km
time	1 hour 15 minutes (not including castle/ museum visits)
terrain	Paved roads and paths, one flight of steps, some hills including one very steep downhill cobbled street.

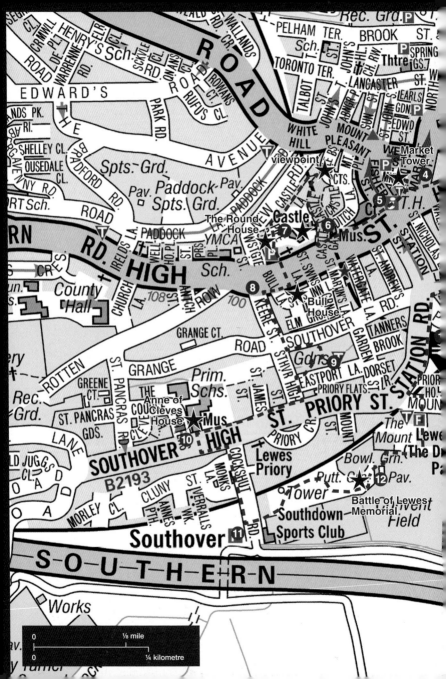

PHOENIX IND. EST.

PHOENIX PL.

A26

PHOENIX CAUSEWAY

THOMAS ST.

MALL

Underline House

Res. (cov.)

Mem.

Cuilfail

Superstore

MALLING ST.

CUILFAIL

EASTGATE

Brewery

WHARF

ENGLISH'S PAS.

P

MALLING ST.

HARVE WY.

P

TUNNEL SOUTH

Bus Sta

EASTGATE ST.

ST.

FILLERS PAS.

BROO

MAN'S

Lib.

CLIFFE

T

P

RAILWAY

2

HIGH

ST.

FOUNDRY YD.

MORRIS

RGE LA.

SOUTH

CHAPEL

HILL

STREET

Court R.

COURT ROAD

RD.

FRIAR'S WK.

GREYFRIARS CT.

Cliffe

FOUNDRY LA.

TIMBERYARD LA.

SOUTH P. CLEE

TIMBER YD.

HILLMAN COTTS.

HILLMAN CL.

Rowing Club

Lewes Railway Land
Local Nature Reserve

Cliffe Cut

RIVER

OUSE

A26

Inland
Rev.

ROYAL SUSSEX CT.

Sussex Downs
College

Caburn
Ho.

ROAD

**Lewes
Leisure
Centre**

Coll.

HAM LA.

Ten. Cts.

Priory
Sch.

**Lewes
Athletics
Track**

HAM

LANE

Playing Field

The Cockshut

Sewage
Works

SOUTHERHAM

A27

B—Y—P—A—S—S

SOUTHERHAM

STREET

SOUTHERHAM
RBT.

ewes

❶ Leaving Lewes Station, turn right, then after the bridge turn right onto Lansdown Place and continue as this street turns into Friar's Walk. At the traffic light junction, turn right into the pedestrianized High Street. Cross the bridge over the River Ouse and note on the left Harvey's Brewery ★ , the oldest independent brewery in Sussex, and the old wharves on the right, a reminder of the town's past as an inland port.

❷ Continue along the lively Cliffe High Street – until 1881 Cliffe was a separate village. Towards the end of the street note the 12th-century St Thomas à Becket Church. At the end, continue ahead to Chapel Hill with its pretty cottages. After about 110 yards (100 metres), before the steep rise, turn round and retrace your steps back along Cliffe High Street and return to the Lewes side of the bridge.

❸ When you reach the traffic lights, continue ahead up the hill on the right-hand side of the road. At the top junction with the war memorial, carefully cross the road and turn right down Market Street. Immediately turn left through the brick arch to enter Market Tower ★ an 18th-century clock tower, where there are information boards about Lewes resident Thomas Paine, 'father of the American Revolution'.

❹ Retrace your steps and turn right out of the Market Tower and keep right to continue along High Street with the red brick Town Hall on your right. At the far end of the Town Hall note the railings around some stone steps which led to the undercroft where 17 people were held before being executed on the street for their Protestant faith during the reign of Queen Mary in the 1550s.

❺ Continue over the traffic lights. On your left is the White Hart Hotel with a plaque remembering the debating club where Thomas Paine formulated his world-changing political theories. After about 220 yards (200 metres), turn right into Castle Gate. Here you can see the high keep of Lewes Castle ★ , which can be visited (entry fee payable) with a museum opposite.

❻ Walk up beneath two impressive gatehouses (1100 and mid-1300s respectively) and past the bowling green (originally part of the castle). At the end of the road, continue ahead to the viewpoint ★ , which has information boards about the Battle of Lewes. Then, take the footpath left along the line of the old castle wall. When you emerge onto a road, turn left, then almost immediately turn left again up some steps and into another footpath, Pipe Passage.

7 On your right, note the hexagonal cottage, The Round House ★, formerly the base of a windmill and home to writer Virginia Woolf in 1919. At the end of the footpath be aware of pedestrians and cars as you emerge onto the narrow pavement of High Street. Look across the road to the 15th-century Bull House ★, where Thomas Paine lived (1768–1774). Carefully cross the road and turn right.

8 Take the next left down Keere Street. Be cautious on the steep cobbles, particularly when wet. At the bottom turn left and cross to the right-hand pavement of Southover Road. At the end of the stone buildings, look for a gap in the wall on your right and enter Southover Grange Gardens. Follow the path then turn right to the lawns and the view of the 16th-century stone Southover Grange, childhood home of diarist John Evelyn, now a Register Office.

9 Turning right to face the house, head for the arch on the left-hand side of the lawn taking you through to a walled garden. Follow this path to finally leave the gardens through another arch in the far corner. Walk up this short section of road to the mini-roundabout then turn right along Southover High Street.

10 After about 220 yards (200 metres) you come to Anne of Cleves House ★. Although the fourth wife of King Henry VIII never lived here, she was given it as part of the settlement after their marriage was annulled. Today it is a museum of Tudor domestic life and local history. Leaving the house, cross the road and turn left to head back along Southover High Street on the right-hand side. Turn right down Cockshut Road, taking care on the sections with no pavement.

11 After the railway bridge, take the path on the left, taking you into Lewes Priory Park. Follow the main path, and, as you approach the priory ruins, follow the lower path as it bears rights between the buildings (the former dormitory and toilet block). Before the Battle of Lewes in 1264, King Henry III used the priory as a base, and the battle is commemorated with a helmet-inspired sculpture ★ on the far side of the park.

12 Past the sculpture, leave Lewes Priory Park by following the path up the hill then right into some playing fields. Keep left and follow the path that runs along the wall. At the end of the wall turn left. On your right is the home of Lewes Football Club and on your left is The Mount, a curious artificial hill with many theories surrounding its origins, but it was probably built sometime around 1600 as a folly. At the end of the path, cross Mountfield Road, turn left then immediately right to take you back to the station.

images